DATE DUE

JE 5 '87	JA 15 93	
F 26 8		
MR 3	JA 27	
MR 2 90	FE 21 92	JA 5 86
MR 2 90	JA 20 93	MR 1 1 96
MR 2 90		
Renew		
	E 10 '9	
FE 19 9	MR 5 '9	
F 8	OE 1 1 03	
AP 5 9		

Modern Critical Interpretations

Herman Melville's
Moby-Dick

Modern Critical Interpretations

These and other titles in preparation

Herman Melville's
Moby-Dick

Edited and with an introduction by

Harold Bloom
Sterling Professor of the Humanities
Yale University

Chelsea House Publishers ◇ *1986*
NEW YORK ◇ NEW HAVEN ◇ PHILADELPHIA

© 1986 by Chelsea House Publishers, a division of Chelsea
House Educational Communications, Inc.
   133 Christopher Street, New York, NY 10014
   345 Whitney Avenue, New Haven, CT 06511
   5014 West Chester Pike, Edgemont, PA 19028

Introduction © 1986 by Harold Bloom

Printed and bound in the United States of America

∞ The paper used in this publication meets the minimum
requirements of the American National Standard for
Permanence of Paper for Printed Library Materials,
Z39.48–1984.

Library of Congress Cataloging-in-Publication Data
Herman Melville's Moby Dick.
   (Modern critical interpretations)
   Bibliography: p.
   Includes index.
      Summary: A collection of eight critical essays on
   Melville's novel "Moby Dick," arranged in chronological
   order of publication.
      1. Melville, Herman, 1819–1891.   Moby Dick.
   [1. Melville, Herman, 1819–1891.   Moby Dick.
   2. American literature—History and criticism]
   I. Bloom, Harold.   II. Series.
   PS2384.M62H38 1986   813'.3   86-8303
   ISBN 1-55546-010-0 (alk. paper.)

Contents

Editor's Note

This book gathers together a representative selection of what its editor considers to be the most useful criticism available on Herman Melville's *Moby-Dick*, arranged in the chronological order of its original publication. I am grateful to Mary Quaintance for her skill as a researcher.

The editor's introduction begins by viewing *Moby-Dick* retrospectively, through "The Bell Tower," one of the remarkable stories in Melville's *The Piazza Tales*, published in 1856, five years after *Moby-Dick*. My essay then applies "The Bell-Tower," as a text evidencing a demiurgical pain and guilt, to *Moby-Dick*, in order to suggest how strong the Gnostic or antithetical strain is in what might be called the negative Sublime of our national epic.

Charles Olson's seminal reverie, *Call Me Ishmael*, rightly begins the chronological sequence, since Olson has fathered most subsequent criticism of *Moby-Dick*. His visionary reverie is followed here by Henry A. Murray's psychological account of Captain Ahab, an analysis that finds Ahab to be solipsistic and nihilistic, conclusions that are challenging but rather dubious, in my judgment. A very different reading, also psychologically founded, is offered in David Simpson's discussion of phallic symbolism and fetishism, which finds in the White Whale "the fetish who compulsively attracts and inexorably disappoints, only to attract again."

Ishmael becomes the center in Rowland A. Sherrill's study of Melville's mode of self-transcendence, in which the transcendent dimension always retains its radical otherness, and so cannot be deciphered. A very different kind of criticism, meditating upon genre, is exemplified by Bert Bender's inquiry into what is uniquely American about the lyricism of Melville's finest novel. Another kind of criticism, reflecting upon the diverse languages of *Moby-Dick*, is strongly represented by Louise K. Barnett's essay, which distinguishes Ahab's mode of speech from Ishmael's, while refusing to identify Ishmael's with that of Melville himself.

Frank G. Novak, Jr., concerning himself with the metaphysics of the Sublime in *Moby-Dick*, concludes that the opposition between beauty and terror in the book has its Emersonian affinities. Finally, P. Adams Sitney radically advances the analysis of *Moby-Dick* with a poignant reading of its great chapter 132, "The Symphony," in which the Gnostic quester of a hero asks himself, and us, the unanswerable question: "Is Ahab, Ahab?"

Introduction

Melville's *The Piazza Tales* was published in 1856, five years after *Moby-Dick*. Two of the six tales—"Bartleby, The Scrivener" and "Benito Cereno"—are commonly and rightly accepted among Melville's strongest works, together with *Moby-Dick* and (rather more tenuously) *The Confidence-Man* and *Billy Budd, Sailor.* Two others—"The Encantadas, or Enchanted Isles" and "The Bell-Tower"—seem to me even better, being equal to the best moments in *Moby-Dick*. Two of the *The Piazza Tales* are relative trifles: "The Piazza" and "The Lightning-Rod Man." A volume of novellas with four near-masterpieces is an extraordinary achievement, but particularly poignant if, like Melville, you had lost your reading public after the early success of *Typee* and *Omoo*, the more equivocal reception of *Mardi*, and the return to a wider audience with *Redburn* and even more with *White-Jacket*. *Moby-Dick* today is, together with *Leaves of Grass* and *Huckleberry Finn*, one of the three candidates for our national epic, but like *Leaves of Grass* it found at first only the one great reader (Hawthorne for Melville, Emerson for Whitman) and almost no popular response. What was left of Melville's early audience was killed off by the dreadful *Pierre*, a year after *Moby-Dick*, and despite various modern salvage attempts *Pierre* certainly is unreadable, in the old-fashioned sense of that now critically abused word. You just cannot get through it, unless you badly want and need to do so.

The best of *The Piazza Tales* show the post-*Pierre* Melville writing for himself, possibly Hawthorne, and a few strangers. Himself the sole support of wife, four children, mother and several sisters, Melville was generally in debt from at least 1855 on, and Hawthorne and Richard Henry Dana, though they tried, could not get the author of *Pierre* appointed to a consulate. In the late 1850s, the tormented and shy Melville attempted the lecture circuit, but as he was neither a pulpit-pounder like Henry Ward Beecher, nor a preternaturally eloquent sage like Ralph Waldo Emerson, he failed rather badly. Unhappily married, mother-ridden, an apparent literary failure; the author of *The Piazza Tales* writes out of the depths. Steeped, as were Carlyle and Ruskin, in the King James Bible, Melville no more believed in the Bible than did Carlyle and Ruskin. But even as *Moby-Dick* found its legitimate and overwhelming precursors in the Bible, Spenser, Shakespeare and Milton, so do *The Piazza Tales*. Melville's rejection of Biblical theology, his almost Gnostic distrust of nature and history alike, finds powerful expression in *The Piazza Tales,* as it did throughout all his later fictional prose and his verse.

II

"The Bell-Tower" is a tale of only fifteen pages but it has such resonance and strength that each rereading gives me the sense that I have experienced a superb short novel. Bannadonna, "the great mechanician, the unblest foundling," seeking to conquer a larger liberty, like Prometheus, instead extended the empire of necessity. His great Bell-Tower, intended to be the noblest in Italy, survives only as "a stone pine," a "black massed stump." It is the new tower of Babel:

> Like Babel's, its base was laid in a high hour of renovated earth, following the second deluge, when the waters of the Dark Ages had dried up, and once more the green appeared. No wonder that, after so long and deep submersion, the jubilant expectation of the race should, as with Noah's sons, soar into Shinar aspiration.
>
> In firm resolve, no man in Europe at that period went beyond Bannadonna. Enriched through commerce with the Levant, the state in which he lived voted to have the noblest Bell-Tower in Italy. His repute assigned him to be architect.
>
> Stone by stone, month by month, the tower rose. Higher, higher; snail-like in pace, but torch or rocket in its pride.
>
> After the masons would depart, the builder, standing alone upon its ever-ascending summit, at close of every day saw that he overtopped still higher walls and trees. He would tarry till a late hour there, wrapped in schemes of other and still loftier piles. Those who of saints' days thronged the spot—hanging to the rude poles of scaffolding, like sailors on yards, or bees on boughs, unmindful of lime and dust, and falling chips of stone— their homage not the less inspired him to self-esteem.

At length the holiday of the Tower came. To the sound of viols, the climax-stone slowly rose in air, and, amid the firing of ordnance, was laid by Bannadonna's hands upon the final course. Then mounting it, he stood erect, alone, with folded arms, gazing upon the white summits of blue inland Alps, and whiter crests of bluer Alps off-shore—sights invisible from the plain. Invisible, too, from thence was that eye he turned below, when, like the cannon booms, came up to him the people's combustions of applause.

That which stirred them so was, seeing with what serenity the builder stood three hundred feet in air, upon an unrailed perch. This none but he durst do. But his periodic standing upon the pile, in each stage of its growth—such discipline had its last result.

We recognize Captain Ahab in Bannadonna, though Ahab has his humanities, and the great mechanician lacks all pathos. Ahab plays out an avenger's tragedy, but Bannadonna's purpose lacks any motivation except pride. His pride presumably is related to the novelist's, and the black stump that is the sole remnant of the Bell-Tower might as well be *Pierre,* little as Melville would have welcomed such an identification. The sexual mortification of the image is palpable, yet adds little to the comprehensiveness of what will become Bannadonna's doom, since that necessarily is enacted as a ritual of castration anyway. Melville's Prometheans, Ahab and Bannadonna, have an overtly Gnostic quarrel with the heavens. Melville's narratives, at their strongest, know implicitly what Kafka asserted with rare explicitness in his great parable:

> The crows maintain that a single crow could destroy the heavens.
> Doubtless that is so, but it proves nothing against the heavens
> for the heavens signify simply: the impossibility of crows.

In Melville, the heavens signify simply: the impossibility of Ahab and of Bannadonna. Ahab is a hunter and not a builder, but to destroy Moby-Dick or to build the Bell-Tower would be to pile up the Tower of Babel and get away with it:

> If it had been possible to build the Tower of Babel without
> ascending it, the work would have been permitted.

Kafka's aphorism would be an apt title for Melville's story, with Bannadonna who has built his tower partly in order to ascend it and to stand "three hundred feet in air, upon an unrailed perch." Kafka could have told Bannadonna that a labyrinth underground would have been better, though of course that too would not have been permitted, since the heavens would have regarded it as the pit of Babel:

> What are you building? — I want to dig a subterranean passage. Some progress must be made. My station up there is much too high.
> We are digging the pit of Babel.

Bannadonna is closest to the most extraordinary of the Kafkan parables concerning the Tower, in which a scholar maintains that the Great Wall of China "alone would provide for the first time in the history of mankind a secure foundation for the new Tower of Babel. First the wall, therefore, and then the tower." The final sentence of "The Great Wall and the Tower of Babel" could have impressed Melville as the best possible commentary upon Bannadonna-Melville, both in his project and his fate:

> There were many wild ideas in people's heads at that time — this scholar's book is only one example — perhaps simply because so many were trying to join forces as far as they could for the achievement of a single aim. Human nature, essentially changeable, unstable as the dust, can endure no restraint; if it binds itself it soon begins to tear madly at its bonds, until it rends everything asunder, the wall, the bonds and its very self.

The fall of Bannadonna commences with the casting of the great bell:

> The unleashed metals bayed like hounds. The workmen shrunk. Through their fright, fatal harm to the bell was dreaded. Fearless as Shadrach, Bannadonna, rushing through the glow, smote the chief culprit with his ponderous ladle. From the smitten part, a splinter was dashed into the seething mass, and at once was melted in.

That single blemish is evidently Melville's personal allegory for whatever sense of guilt, in his own pained judgment, flawed his own achievement, even in *Moby-Dick*. More interesting is Bannadonna's creation of a kind of *golem* or Frankensteinean monster, charmingly called Haman, doubtless in tribute to the villain of the Book of Esther. Haman, intended to be the bell-ringer, is meant also: "as a partial type of an ulterior creature," a titanic helot who would be called Talus, like the rather sinister iron man who wields an iron flail against the rebellious Irish in the savage book 5 of

Spenser's *The Faerie Queene*. But Talus is never created; Haman is quite enough to immolate the ambitious artist, Bannadonna:

> And so, for the interval, he was oblivious of his creature; which, not oblivious of him, and true to its creation, and true to its heedful winding up, left its post precisely at the given moment; along its well-oiled route, slid noiselessly towards its mark; and aiming at the hand of Una, to ring one clangorous note, dully smote the intervening brain of Bannadonna, turned backwards to it; the manacled arms then instantly upspringing to their hovering poise. The falling body clogged the thing's return; so there it stood, still impending over Bannadonna, as if whispering some post-mortem terror. The chisel lay dropped from the hand, but beside the hand; the oil-flask spilled across the iron track.

Which of his own works destroyed Melville? Juxtapose the story's deliberately Addisonian or Johnsonian conclusion with the remarkable stanza in Hart Crane's "The Broken Tower" that it helped inspire, and perhaps a hint emerges, since Crane was a superb interpreter of Melville:

> So the blind slave obeyed its blinder lord; but, in obedience, slew him. So the creator was killed by the creature. So the bell was too heavy for the tower. So that bell's main weakness was where man's blood had flawed it. And so pride went before the fall.

> > The bells, I say, the bells break down their tower;
> > And swing I know not where. Their tongues engrave
> > Membrane through marrow, my long-scattered score
> > Of broken intervals . . . And I, their sexton slave!

Crane is both Bannadonna and Haman, a complex fate darker even than Melville's, who certainly had represented himself as Bannadonna. The Bell-Tower of Bannadonna perhaps was *Pierre* but more likely *Moby-Dick* itself, Melville's "long-scattered score / Of broken intervals" even as *The Bridge* was Hart Crane's. This is hardly to suggest that Haman is Captain Ahab. Yet Melville's "wicked book," as he called *Moby-Dick* in a famous letter to Hawthorne, indeed may have slain something vital in its author, if only in his retrospective consciousness.

III

"Canst thou draw out Leviathan with a hook?," God's taunting question to Job, can be said to be answered by Captain Ahab with a "Yes!" in thunder. Job's God wins, Ahab loses, and the great white Leviathan swims away, harpooned yet towing Ahab with him. But Ahab's extraordinary last speech denies that Moby-Dick is the conquerer:

> I turn my body from the sun. What ho, Tashtego! let me hear thy hammer. Oh! ye three unsurrendered spires of mine; thou uncracked keel; and only god-bullied hull; thou firm deck, and haughty helm, and Pole-pointed prow,—death-glorious ship! must ye then perish, and without me? Am I cut off from the last fond pride of meanest shipwrecked captains? Oh, lonely death on lonely life! Oh, now I feel my topmost greatness lies in my topmost grief. Ho, ho! from all your furthest bounds, pour ye now in, ye bold billows of my whole foregone life, and top this one piled comber of my death! Towards thee I roll, thou all-destroying but unconquering whale; to the last I grapple with thee; from hell's heart I stab at thee; for hate's sake I spit my last breath at thee. Sink all coffins and all hearses to one common pool! and since neither can be mine, let me then tow to pieces, while still chasing thee, though tied to thee, thou damned whale! *Thus,* I give up the spear!

Beyond the allusions — Shakespearean, Miltonic, Byronic — what rings out here is Melville's own grand self-echoing, which is of Father Mapple's sermon as it concludes:

> He drooped and fell away from himself for a moment; then lifting his face to them again, showed a deep joy in his eyes, as he cried out with a heavenly enthusiasm,—"But oh! shipmates! on the starboard hand of every woe, there is a sure delight; and higher the top of that delight, than the bottom of the woe is deep. Is not the main-truck higher than the kelson is low? Delight is to him—a far, far upward, and inward delight—who against the proud gods and commodores of this earth, ever stands forth his own inexorable self. Delight is to him whose strong arms yet support him, when the ship of this base treacherous world has gone down beneath him. Delight is to him, who gives no quarter in the truth, and kills, burns, and destroys all sin though he pluck it out from under the robes of Senators and Judges. Delight,—top-gallant delight is to him, who acknowledges no law or lord, but the Lord his God, and is only a patriot to heaven. Delight is to him, whom all the waves of the billows of the seas

of the boisterous mob can never shake from this sure Keel of the Ages. And eternal delight and deliciousness will be his, who coming to lay him down, can say with his final breath—O Father!—chiefly known to me by Thy rod—mortal or immortal, here I die. I have striven to be Thine, more than to be this world's, or mine own. Yet this is nothing; I leave eternity to Thee; for what is man that he should live out the lifetime of his God?"

Father Mapple's intensity moves from "a sure delight, and higher the top of that delight" through "a far, far upward, and inward delight" on to "Delight,—top-gallant delight is to him," heaven's patriot. Ahab's equal but antithetical intensity proceeds from "unsurrendered spires of mine" through "my topmost greatness lies in my topmost grief" to end in "top this one piled comber of my death." After which the *Pequod* goes down with Tashtego hammering a hawk to the mainmast, an emblem not of being "only a patriot to heaven" but rather of a Satanic dragging of "a living part of heaven along with her." Admirable as Father Mapple is, Ahab is certainly the hero, more Promethean than Satanic, and we need not conclude (as so many critics do) that Melville chooses Mapple's stance over Ahab's. William Faulkner, in 1927, asserted that the book he most wished he had written was *Moby-Dick,* and called Ahab's fate "a sort of Golgotha of the heart become immutable as bronze in the sonority of its plunging ruin," characteristically adding: "There's a death for a man, now."

As Faulkner implied, there is a dark sense in which Ahab intends his Golgotha, like Christ's, to be a vicarious atonement for all of staggering Adam's woes. When Melville famously wrote to Hawthorne: "I have written a wicked book," he was probably quite serious. The common reader does not come to love Ahab, and yet there is a serious disproportion between that reader's awe of, and admiration for, Ahab, and the moral dismissal of the monomaniacal hero by many scholarly critics. Ahab seems to provoke academic critics rather more even than Milton's Satan does. Ishmael, presumably speaking for Melville, consistently emphasizes Ahab's greatness. And so does Ahab himself, as when he confronts the corposants or St. Elmo's fire, in the superb Chapter 119, "The Candles":

Oh! thou clear spirit of clear fire, whom on these seas I as Persian once did worship, till in the sacramental act so burned by thee, that to this hour I bear the scar; I now know thee, thou clear spirit, and I now know that thy right worship is defiance. To neither love nor reverence wilt thou be kind; and e'en for hate thou canst but kill; and all are killed. No fearless fool now fronts thee. I own thy speechless, placeless power; but to the last gasp of my earthquake life will dispute its unconditional, unintegral mastery in me. In the midst of the personified impersonal, a personality stands here. Though but a point at best; whencesoe'er I came; wheresoe'er I go; yet while I earthly live, the queenly personality lives in me, and feels her royal rights. But war is pain, and hate is woe. Come in thy lowest form of love, and I will kneel and kiss thee; but at thy highest, come as mere supernal power; and though thou launchest navies of full-freighted worlds, there's that in here that still remains indifferent. Oh, thou clear spirit, of thy fire thou madest me, and like a true child of fire, I breathe it back to thee.

If Ahab has a religion, it is Persian or rather Parsee, and so Zoroastrian. But Melville has not written a Zoroastrian hymn to the benign light for Ahab to chant. Ahab's invocation is clearly Gnostic in spirit and in substance, since the light is hailed as being both ambiguous and ambivalent. Ahab himself knows that the clear spirit of clear fire is not from the Alien God but from the Demiurge, and he seems to divide the Demiurge into both the "lowest form of love" and the "highest . . . mere supernal power." Against this dialectical or even self-contradictory spirit, Ahab sets himself as personality rather than as moral character: "In the midst of the personified impersonal, a personality stands here." As a personality, Ahab confronts "the personified impersonal," which he astonishingly names as his father, and defies, as knowing less than he, Ahab, knows:

I own thy speechless, placeless power; said I not so? Nor was it wrung from me; nor do I now drop these links. Thou canst blind; but I can then grope. Thou canst consume; but I can then be ashes. Take the homage of these poor eyes, and shutter-hands. I would not take it. The lightning flashes through my skull; mine eye-balls ache and ache; my whole beaten brain seems as beheaded, and rolling on some stunning ground. Oh, oh! Yet blindfold, yet will I talk to thee. Light though thou be, thou leapest out of darkness; but I am darkness leaping out of light, leaping out of thee! The javelins cease; open eyes; see, or not? There burn the flames! Oh, thou magnanimous! now I do glory in my genealogy. But thou art but my fiery father; my sweet mother, I know not. Oh, cruel! what hast thou done with her? There lies my puzzle; but thine is greater. Thou knowest not how came ye, hence callest thyself unbegotten; certainly knowest not thy beginning, hence callest thyself unbegun. I know that of me, which thou knowest not of thyself, oh, thou omnipotent. There is some unsuffusing thing beyond thee, thou clear spirit, to whom all thy eternity is but time, all thy creativeness mechanical. Through thee, thy flaming self, my scorched eyes do dimly see it. Oh, thou foundling fire, thou hermit immemorial, thou too hast thy incommunicable riddle, thy unparticipated grief. Here again with haughty agony, I read my sire. Leap! leap up, and lick the sky! I leap with thee; I burn with thee; would fain be welded with thee; defyingly I worship thee!

The Gnosticism here is explicit and unmistakable, since "some unsuffusing thing beyond thee, thou clear spirit, to whom all thy eternity is but time, all thy creativeness mechanical" is certainly what the Gnostics called the true or alien God, cut off from our cosmos. But who is Ahab's "sweet mother"? Ahab scarcely recognizes a benign aspect of our cosmos, so that his mother, in Gnostic terms, must be the original abyss, preceding the Demiurge's false creation. But, as Melville knew, that motherly abyss, in Gnosticism, is also the forefather or Alien God. Echoing the Gnostics' savage reading of the opening of Genesis, Ahab insinuates that his father, the Demiurge, begat him upon the true God, or abyss, his mother. Rebelling (though equivocally) against his father, Ahab proudly asserts his mother's knowledge of origins against his father's ignorance. When Ahab cries out that he wishes to be welded with his father, we rightly should flinch, because that is the book's true wickedness. Ahab, like Bannadonna, like Melville himself, desires to be one with the Demiurge.

IV

The visionary center of *Moby-Dick,* and so of all Melville, as critics always have recognized, is chapter 42, "The Whiteness of the Whale." It is Ishmael's meditation, and not Ahab's, and yet how far is it from Ahab? Ishmael is himself half a Gnostic:

Though in many of its aspects this visible world seems formed in love, the invisible spheres were formed in fright.

Closer to Carlyle than to Emerson, this extraordinary sentence is the prelude to the final paragraph of Ishmael's reverie:

But not yet have we solved the incantation of this whiteness, and learned why it appeals with such power to the soul; and more strange and far more portentous—why, as we have seen, it is at once the most meaning symbol of spiritual things, nay, the very veil of the Christian's Deity; and yet should be as it is, the intensifying agent in things the most appalling to mankind.

Is it that by its indefiniteness it shadows forth the heartless voids and immensities of the universe, and thus stabs us from behind with the thought of annihilation, when beholding the white depths of the milky way? Or is it, that as in essence whiteness is not so much a color as the visible absence of color, and at the same time the concrete of all colors; is it for these reasons that there is such a dumb blankness, full of meaning, in a wide landscape of snows—a colorless, all-color of atheism from which we shrink? And when we consider that other theory of the natural philosophers, that all other earthly hues—every stately or lovely emblazoning—the sweet tinges of sunset skies and woods; yea, and the gilded velvets of butterflies, and the butterfly cheeks of young girls; all these are but subtile deceits, not actually inherent in substances, but only laid on from without; so that all deified Nature absolutely paints like the harlot, whose allurements cover nothing but the charnel-house within; and when we proceed further, and consider that the mystical cosmetic which produces every one of her hues, the great principle of light, for ever remains white or colorless in itself, and if operating without medium upon matter, would touch all objects, even tulips and roses, with its own blank tinge—pondering all this, the palsied universe lies before us a leper; and like wilful travellers in Lapland, who refuse to wear colored and coloring glasses upon their eyes, so the wretched infidel gazes himself blind at the monumental white shroud that wraps all the prospect around him. And of all these things the Albino whale was the symbol. Wonder ye then at the fiery hunt?

Ishmael's "visible absence of color" becomes the trope of whiteness, "a dumb blankness," similar to its descendant in the beach-scene of Wallace Stevens's "The Auroras of Autumn":

> Here, being visible is being white,
> Is being of the solid of white, the accomplishment
> Of an extremist in an exercise . . .
>
> The season changes. A cold wind chills the beach.
> The long lines of it grow longer, emptier,
> A darkness gathers though it does not fall.

And the whiteness grows less vivid on the wall.
The man who is walking turns blankly on the sand.

Melville and Stevens alike shrink from "a colorless, all-color of atheism," not because they are theists, but precisely because they both believe in and fear the Demiurge. When Ishmael cries out: "Wonder ye then at the fiery hunt?" he refutes all those critics, moral and psychoanalytic, who condemn Ahab as being immoral or insane. It was Melville, after all, who wrote two memorable quatrains, in the mode of Blake, which he entitled "Fragments of a Lost Gnostic Poem of the 12th Century":

Found a family, build a state,
The pledged event is still the same:
Matter in end will never abate
His ancient brutal claim.

Indolence is heaven's ally here,
And energy the child of hell:
The Good Man pouring from his pitcher clear,
But brims the poisoned well.

There the Gnosticism is overt, and we are left a little cold, since even a heretical doctrine strikes us as tendentious, as having too clear a design upon us. Perhaps "The Bell-Tower" is a touch tendentious also. *Moby-Dick*, despite its uneven rhetoric, despite its excessive debt to Shakespeare, Milton and Byron, is anything but tendentious. It remains the darker half of our national epic, complementing *Leaves of Grass* and *Huckleberry Finn*, works of more balance certainly, but they do not surpass or eclipse Melville's version of darkness visible.

Call Me Ishmael

Charles Olson

I take SPACE to be the central fact to man born in America, from Folsom cave to now. I spell it large because it comes large here. Large, and without mercy.

It is geography at bottom, a hell of wide land from the beginning. That made the first American story (Parkman's): exploration.

Something else than a stretch of earth—seas on both sides, no barriers to contain as restless a thing as Western man was becoming in Columbus' day. That made Melville's story (part of it).

PLUS a harshness we still perpetuate, a sun like a tomahawk, small earthquakes but big tornadoes and hurrikans, a river north and south in the middle of the land running out the blood.

The fulcrum of America is the Plains, half sea half land, a high sun as metal and obdurate as the iron horizon, and a man's job to square the circle.

Some men ride on such space, others have to fasten themselves like a tent stake to survive. As I see it Poe dug in and Melville mounted. They are the alternatives.

Americans still fancy themselves such democrats. But their triumphs are of the machine. It is the only master of space the average person ever knows, oxwheel to piston, muscle to jet. It gives trajectory.

To Melville it was not the will to be free but the will to overwhelm nature that lies at the bottom of us as individuals and a people. Ahab is no democrat. Moby-Dick, antagonist, is only king of natural force, resource.

I am interested in a Melville who decided sometime in 1850 to write a book about the whaling industry and what happened to a man in command of one of the most successful machines Americans had perfected up to that time—the whaleship.

This captain, Ahab by name, knew space. He rode it across seven seas. He was an able skipper, what the fishing people I was raised with call a highliner. Big catches: he brought back holds barrel full of the oil of the sperm, the light of American and European communities up to the middle of the 19th century.

This Ahab had gone wild. The object of his attention was something unconscionably big and white. He had become a specialist: he had all space concentrated into the form of a whale called Moby-Dick. And he assailed it as Columbus an ocean, LaSalle a continent, the Donner Party their winter Pass.

I am interested in a Melville who was long-eyed enough to understand the Pacific as part of our geography, another West, prefigured in the Plains, antithetical.

The beginning of man was salt sea, and the perpetual reverberation of that great ancient fact, constantly renewed in the unfolding of life in every human individual, is the important single fact about Melville. Pelagic.

He had the tradition in him, deep, in his brain, his words, the salt beat of his blood. He had the sea of himself in a vigorous, stricken way, as Poe the street. It enabled him to draw up from Shakespeare. It made Noah, and Moses, contemporary to him. History was ritual and repetition when Melville's imagination was at its own proper beat.

It was an older sense than the European man's, more to do with magic than culture. Magic which, in contrast to worship, is all black. For magic has one purpose: compel men or non-human forces to do one's will. Like Ahab, American, one aim: lordship over nature.

I am willing to ride Melville's image of man, whale and ocean to find in him prophecies, lessons he himself would not have spelled out. A hundred years gives us an advantage. For Melville was as much larger than himself as Ahab's hate. He was a plunger. He knew how to take a chance.

The man made a mess of things. He got all balled up with Christ. He made a white marriage. He had one son die of tuberculosis, the other shoot himself. He only rode his own space once—*Moby-Dick*. He had to be wild or he was nothing in particular. He had to go fast, like an American, or he was all torpor. Half horse half alligator.

Melville took an awful licking. He was bound to. He was an original, aboriginal. A beginner. It happens that way to the dreaming men it takes to discover America: Columbus and LaSalle won, and then lost her to the competent. Daniel Boone loved her earth. Harrod tells the story of coming upon Boone one day far to the west in Kentucky of where Harrod thought any white man had ever been. He heard sound he couldn't place, crept forward to a boulder and there in a blue grass clearing was Boone alone singing to himself. Boone died west of the Mississippi, in his own country criminal—"wanted," a bankrupt of spirit and land.

Beginner—and interested in beginnings. Melville had a way of reaching back through time until he got history pushed back so far he turned time into space. He was like a migrant backtrailing to Asia, some Inca trying to find a lost home.

We are the last "first" people. We forget that. We act big, misuse our land, ourselves. We lose our own primary.

Melville went back, to discover us, to come forward. He got as far as *Moby-Dick*.

Ortega y Gasset puts it that the man of antiquity, before he did anything, took a step like the bullfighter who leaps back in order to deliver the mortal thrust.

Whitman appears, because of his notation of the features of American life and his conscious identification of himself with the people, to be more the poet. But Melville had the will. He was homeless in his land, his society, his self.

Logic and classification had led civilization toward man, away from space. Melville went to space to probe and find man. Early men did the same: poetry, language and the care of myth, as Fenollosa says, grew up together. Among the Egyptians Horus was the god of writing and the god of the moon, one figure for both, a WHITE MONKEY.

In place of Zeus, Odysseus, Olympus we have had Caesar, Faust, the City. The shift was from man as a group to individual man. Now, in spite of the corruption of myth by fascism, the swing is out and back. Melville is one who began it.

He had a pull to the origin of things, the first day, the first man, the unknown sea, Betelgeuse, the buried continent. From passive places his imagination sprang a harpoon.

He sought prime. He had the coldness we have, but he warmed himself by first fires after Flood. It gave him the power to find the lost past of America, the unfound present, and make a myth, *Moby-Dick*, for a people of Ishmaels.

The thing got away from him. It does, from us. We made AHAB, the WHITE WHALE, and lose them. We let John Henry go, Negro, worker, hammering man:

> He lied down his hammer an' he died.

Whitman we have called our greatest voice because he gave us hope. Melville is the truer man. He lived intensely his people's wrong, their guilt. But he remembered the first dream. The *White Whale* is more accurate than *Leaves of Grass*. Because it is America, all of her space, the malice, the root.

WHAT LIES UNDER

Melville prepared the way for *Moby-Dick* by ridiculing, in 1850, the idea that the literary genius in America would be, like Shakespeare, "a writer of dramas." This was his proposition:

> great geniuses are parts of the times, they themselves are the times, and possess a corresponding colouring.

Melville raised his times up when he got them into *Moby-Dick* and they held firm in his schema:

> e.g. his *crew*, a "people," Clootz and Tom Paine's people, all races and colors functioning together, a forecastle reality of Americans not yet a dream accomplished by the society;
>
> e.g. his *job on the whaling industry*, a problem in the resolution of forces solved with all forces taken account of: (1) OWNERS Bildad and Peleg (Aunt Charity interested party); (2) Ahab, hard MASTER; (3) the MEN, and TECHNOLOGY, killer boat, tryworks and underdeck storage of yield permitting four-year voyage.

We forget the part the chase of the whale played in American economy. It started from a shortage of fats and oils. The Indian had no cattle, the colonist not enough. It was the same with pigs and goats. Red and white alike had to use substitutes. It accounts for the heavy slaughter of the passenger pigeon and the curlew, plentiful birds; and the slaughter of the buffalo.

The Indians appear to have taken shore whales from an early time. The Makahs around Cape Flattery knew tricks only the present day Norwegian whalers have applied. They blew up seal skins to slow the run of a wounded whale like a sea anchor and to float the dead whale when heavier than water.

The American Indian continued to be a skilled part of the industry down to its end, a miserably paid tool. Melville had reason to name his ship *Pequod* and to make the Gayhead Tashteego one of his three harpooneers.

COMBUSTION. All whales yield oil. Most of the oil is a true fat, a glyceride of the fatty acids. Unlike the Indians the settlers did not find it edible. They boiled the blubber down for tallow. In addition to this fat, commonly called whale oil, the sperm whale and the bottlenose yield a solid wax called spermaceti and a liquid wax called sperm oil. The spermaceti wax is contained in the cavity of the head (vide chp. CISTERN AND BUCKETS, *Moby-Dick*), and in the bones.

Economic historians, lubbers, fail to heft the industry in American economic life up to the Civil War. (In 1859 petroleum was discovered in Pennsylvania. Kerosene, petroleum, and paraffin began rapidly to replace whale oil, sperm oil, and spermaceti wax as illuminating oil, lubricants, and raw materials for candles.)

Whaling expanded at a time when agriculture not industry was the base of labor and when foreign not domestic commerce was the base of trade. A few facts:

> by 1833, 70,000 persons and $70,000,000 were tied up in whaling and such associated crafts as shipbuilding, sail-lofts, smiths to make toggle irons, the thieving outfitters, their agents and the whores of ports like New Bedford;

> by 1844 (peak years roughly 1840-1860) the figure is up to $120,000,000, whaling competes successfully in attracting capital to itself with such opening industries as textiles and shoes, and the export of whale products—one-forth of the catch—is third to meat products and lumber.

A NECESSARY DISSOCIATION: the notion that the China trade and clipper ships made and made up the maritime America which went down as did agrarian America before land and finance speculation, hard metal industry.

The China trade was, economically, distribution, appeared after England closed the West Indies to our rum merchants following the Revolution. It was the way the smugglers, themselves the answer to England's pre-Revolutionary restrictions, went straight.

Whaling was production, as old as the colonies and, in capital and function, forerunner to a later America, with more relation to Socony than to clippers and the China trade.

As early as 1688 there is a record at Boston of a New York brig petitioning Governor Andross for permission to set out "upon a fishing design about the Bohames Islands, And Cap florida, for sperma Coeti whales and Racks."

This was new to whaling, BRAND NEW, American. A FIRST. All the way back to French and Spanish Basques of the Middle Ages it had been cold water whales, the black, right or Greenland whales of northern waters, which had been hunted. But the Yankees had discovered that the Sperm whale had the finest oil and brought the biggest price.

They went after it. And it led them into all the oceans. And gave whaling its leading role in making the Pacific the American lake the navy now, after a lapse of 100 years, has been about the business of certifying.

> A FACT: whale logbooks are today furnishing sea lawyers first claims to islands—the flag & all that;
>
> for whaler as pioneer, cf. chp. THE ADVOCATE, *Moby-Dick*.

You will also discover in that chapter Melville's figures on the value of the industry. Compare to mine above. Thus:

> we whalemen of America now outnumber all the rest of the banded whalemen in the world; sail a navy of upward of seven hundred vessels; manned by eighteen thousand men; yearly consuming 4,000,000 dollars; the ships worth, at the time of sailing, $20,000,000; and every year reporting into our harbours a well-reaped harvest of $7,000,000.

About this outnumbering: of 900 whaling vessels of all nations in 1846, 735 were American.

All this is by way of CORRECTION. I don't intend to dish up cold pork. There are histories of whaling if you are interested. BUT no study weighs the industry in the scale of the total society. What you get is this:

many of the earliest industrial fortunes were built on the "blessing" of the whale fishery!

TWO INTERPOLATIONS. Melville did not know Number 1. Maybe somewhere he does point out Number 2. For he was wide. Add to his knowledge of whaling:

merchant marine	(read *Redburn*)
the Navy	(ditto *White-Jacket*)
assorted carriers of the Pacific	(*Omoo, Mardi,* etc.)
and the Spanish	(by all means read "Benito Cereno" and "The Encantadas," the finest things outside *Moby-Dick*)

Interpolation 1

1762: the colonies still very English, so much so they have little to do with one another, face and act toward London.

Rhode Island: makers of spermaceti candles meet and make covenant to raise the price of wax candles—and keep it raised, it goes without saying. The first American TRUST.

Name: The United Company of Spermaceti Chandlers.

Importance: "shows how colonial boundaries were being eliminated in the minds of the moneyed groups as contrasted with the as yet extremely provincial outlook and provincial patriotism of the smaller people of town and country."

I'm putting a stress Melville didn't on whaling as *industry*. Cutting out the glory: a book *Moby-Dick* turns out to be its glory. We still are soft about our industries, wonder-eyed. What's important is the energy they are a clue to, the drive in the people. The things made are OK, too, some of them. But the captains of industry ain't worth the powder etc. Take the Revolution so long as we're on the subject: whose revolution was it but the "moneyed groups' "; Breed's Hill two weeks after Lexington and it was all over for the "smaller people" until Jefferson gave them another chance.

Don't think whaling was any different from any other American industry. The first men in it, the leaders, explorers, were WORKERS. The money and the glory came later, on top with the exploiters. And the force went down, stayed where it always does, at the underpaid bottom. Where the worker is after the leader is gone.

Whaling started, like so many American industries, as a collective, communal affair. See any history of Sag Harbor or Nantucket. And as late as 1850 there were still skippers to remember the days when they knew the fathers of every man in their crew. But it was already a sweated industry by the time Melville was a hand on a lay (1841–43).

THE TRICK—then as now:

> reduce labor costs lower than worker's efficiency—during the 1840's and '50's it cost the owners 15¢ to 30¢ a day to feed each crew member

> combine inefficient workers and such costs by maintaining lowest wages and miserable working conditions—vide TYPEE, early chps., and *Omoo,* same.

THE RESULT: by the 1840's the crews were the bottom dogs of all nations and all races. Of the 18,000 men (Melville above) *one-half* ranked as green hands and more than *two-thirds* deserted every voyage.

There were so many Pacific natives like Queequeg, the second colored harpooneer, that a section of Nantucket came to be known as New Guinea.

There were so many Portuguese from the Islands that a section of New Bedford was called Fayal.

The third of Melville's harpooneers was the imperial African Negro Ahasuerus Daggoo.

> For bottom dogs made pretty SEE the balletic chapter called MIDNIGHT, FORECASTLE, in *Moby-Dick.*

I insert here a document of our history left out of the published works of Herman Melville. It was written at the same time as *Moby-Dick* and is headed:

> *"What became of the ship's company of the whaleship 'Acushnet,' according to Hubbard who came home in her (more than a four years' voyage) and who visited me at Pittsfield in 1850."*

> *Captain Pease*—retired & lives ashore at the Vineyard
> *Raymond,* 1st Mate—had a fight with the Captain & went ashore
>   at Payta
> *Hall,* 2nd Mate came home & went to California
> *3rd Mate,* Portuguese, went ashore at Payta

Boatsteerer Brown, Portuguese, either ran away or killed at Ropo
  one of the Marquesas
Smith went ashore at Santa coast of Peru, afterwards committed
  suicide at Mobile
Barney boatsteerer came home
Carpenter went ashore at Mowee half dead with disreputable
  disease

The Crew:
Tom Johnson, black, went ashore at Mowee half dead (ditto) &
  died at the hospital
Reed—mulatto—came home
Blacksmith—ran away at St. Francisco
Backus—little black—Do
Bill Green—after various attempts at running away, came home
  in the end
The Irishman ran away at Salango, coast of Columbia
Wright went ashore half dead at the Marquesas
John Adams & Jo Portuguese came home
The old cook came home
Haynes ran away aboard of a Sidney ship
Little Jack—came home
Grant—young fellow—went ashore half dead, spitting blood, at
  Oahu
Murray went ashore, shunning fight, at Rio Janeiro
The Cooper—came home

Melville himself is a case in point. He deserted the *Acushnet,* his first
whaleship, at the Marquesas. He was one of eleven mutineers aboard his
second, a Sydney ship the *Lucy Ann,* at Tahiti. Nothing is known of his
conduct on the third, except that he turned up after it, ashore, at Honolulu.

So if you want to know why Melville nailed us in *Moby-Dick,* consider
whaling. Consider whaling as FRONTIER, and INDUSTRY. A product
wanted, men got it: big business. The Pacific as sweatshop, Man, led,
against the biggest damndest creature nature uncorks. The whaleship as
factory, the whaleboat the precision instrument. The 1840's: the New West
in the saddle and Melville No. 20 of a rough and bastard crew. Are they
the essentials?

BIG? Melville may never have seen the biggest of whales, the blue, the principal kill of the present day. He reaches his full size, 100 feet, at 11 years, lives 20 to 25 years, and weighs 150 tons—or four times the estimated weight of the biggest prehistoric monster and equal to the weight of 37 elephants or 150 fat oxen.

There are two classes of whale: the baleen and the toothed whale. The blue is a baleen. Melville was satisfied with the biggest of the toothed whales, the sperm.

Whales have lungs. To breathe they come to the surface about every half hour. It is this fact that makes them vulnerable to attack by the only important enemy they have—the whaleman.

Melville didn't put it all on the surface of *Moby-Dick*. You'll find the frontier all right, and Andrew Jackson regarded as heavyweight champion (READ end of first KNIGHTS AND SQUIRES chapter for finest rhetoric of democracy). And the technic of an industry analyzed, scrupulously described. But no economics. Jefferson and John Adams observed that in their young days very few men had thought about "government," there were very few writers on "government." Yes, the year *Moby-Dick* was being finished Marx was writing letters to the N.Y. *Daily Tribune*. But Melville
. . . . . .

SOME NECESSARY ECOLOGY. With his baleen the blue whale strains out of the water and eats KRILL. Krill is a shrimplike fish which itself feeds on floating green diatoms. These algae develop in summer in the neighborhood of drift ice.

> *color:* krill spawn at the border of arctic and antarctic ice. The
> offspring drift with the currents toward the equator. They
> are in such abundance they turn the waters pink.

The sperm whale feeds on cuttlefish, particularly on the GIANT SQUID which grows to a 33-foot spread of tentacles and an arm length of 21 feet. Compare *Moby-Dick,* LIX, SQUID. The squid lives on big prawn and small fish, and to catch him the whale dives into depths of several hundred fathom. The struggle leaves sores and marks of the armed suckers on the whale's skin around the mouth.
. . . . . . what counts, Melville had, the *experience,* what lies under. And his own force to resolve the forces.

Interpolation No. 2
Quote. The American whaling era—in contrast to the
Basque, French, Dutch and English—

developed independently
concentrated on different species of whale
covered all seas including the Arctic
yielded on a larger scale than in any other country or group of countries before.

Unquote. . . .

SHAKESPEARE, OR THE DISCOVERY OF *MOBY-DICK*

Moby-Dick was two books written between February, 1850 and August, 1851.

The first book did not contain Ahab.

It may not, except incidentally, have contained Moby-Dick.

On the 7th of August, 1850, the editor Evert Duyckinck reported to
his brother:

Melville has a new book mostly done, a romantic, fanciful &
most literal & most enjoyable presentment of the Whale Fishery—something quite new.

It is not surprising that Melville turned to whaling in February, 1850,
on his return from a trip to England to sell his previous book, *White-Jacket.*
It was the last of the materials his sea experience offered him.

He had used his adventures among the South Sea islands in *Typee*
(1846) and *Omoo* (1847). He had gone further in the vast archipelago of
Mardi, written in 1847 and 1848, to map the outlines of his vision of life.
The books of 1849, *Redburn* and *White-Jacket,* he had based on his experiences
aboard a merchant ship and a man-of-war. The whaling voyage in the
Acushnet was left.

There is no evidence that Melville had decided on the subject before
he started to write in February. On the contrary. Melville's reading is a
gauge of him, at all points of his life. He was a skald, and knew how to
appropriate the work of others. He read to write. Highborn stealth, Edward
Dahlberg calls originality, the act of a cutpurse Autolycus who makes his
thefts as invisible as possible. Melville's books batten on other men's books.
Yet he bought no books on whaling among the many volumes purchased
in England on his trip and soon after his return Putnam's, the publishers,
were picking up in London for him such things as Thomas Beale's *The
Natural History of the Sperm Whale.*

He went at it as he had his last two books, "two jobs," as he called

Redburn and *White-Jacket* in a letter to his father-in-law, "which I have done for money—being forced to it, as other men are to sawing wood." He had a family to support.

By May it was half done. So he told Richard Henry Dana in a letter on the 1st, the only other information of the first Moby-Dick which has survived. The book was giving Melville trouble. Referring to it as "the 'whaling voyage,' " he writes:

> It will be a strange sort of a book, I fear; blubber is blubber you know; tho you may get oil out of it, the poetry runs as hard as sap from a frozen maple tree;—& to cook the thing up, one must needs throw in a little fancy, which from the nature of the thing, must be ungainly as the gambols of the whales themselves. Yet I mean to give the truth of the thing, spite of this.

That's the record of Moby-Dick No. 1, as it stands. There is nothing on why, in the summer of 1850, Melville changed his conception of the work and, on something "mostly done" on August 7th, spent another full year until, in August, 1851, he had created what we know as *Moby-Dick or, The Whale.*

"Dollars damn me." Melville had the bitter thing of men of originality, the struggle between money and me. It was on him, hard, in the spring of 1850. He says as much in the Dana letter: "I write these books of mine almost entirely for 'lucre'—by the job, as a wood-sawyer saws wood," repeating on Moby-Dick what he had said about *Redburn* and *White-Jacket.*

He knew the cost if he let his imagination loose. He had taken his head once, with *Mardi.* In this new work on whaling he felt obliged as he had, after *Mardi,* with *Redburn* and *White-Jacket,* "to refrain from writing the kind of book I would wish to."

He would give the truth of the thing, spite of this, yes. His head was lifted to Dana as it was to his father-in-law seven months earlier. He did his work clean. *Exs: Redburn* and *White-Jacket.* "In writing these two books I have not repressed myself much—so far as *they* are concerned; but have spoken pretty much as I feel."

There was only one thing in the spring of 1850 which he did not feel he could afford to do: "So far as I am individually concerned, & independent of my pocket, it is my earnest desire to write those sort of books which are said to 'fail.' "

In the end, in *Moby-Dick,* he did. Within three months he took his head again. Why?

Through May he continued to try to do a quick book for the market: "all my books are botches." Into June he fought his materials: "blubber is blubber." Then something happened. What, Melville tells:

> I somehow cling to the strange fancy, that, in all men hiddenly reside certain wondrous, occult properties—as in some plants and minerals—which by some happy but very rare accident (as bronze was discovered by the melting of the iron and brass at the burning of Corinth) may chance to be called forth here on earth.

When? Melville is his own tell-tale: he wrote these words in July, 1850. They occur in an article he did for Duyckinck's magazine. He gave it the title HAWTHORNE AND HIS MOSSES, WRITTEN BY A VIRGINIAN SPENDING A JULY IN VERMONT.

The subject is Hawthorne, Shakespeare and Herman Melville. It is a document of Melville's rights and perceptions, his declaration of the freedom of a man to fail. Within a matter of days after it was written (July 18 ff.), Melville had abandoned the account of the Whale Fishery and gambled it and himself with Ahab and the White Whale.

The *Mosses* piece is a deep and lovely thing. The spirit is asweep, as in the book to come. The confusion of May is gone. Melville is charged again. *Moby-Dick* is already shadowed in the excitement over genius, and America as a subject for genius. You can feel Ahab in the making, Ahab of "the globular brain and ponderous heart," so much does Melville concern himself with the distinction between the head and the heart in Hawthorne and Shakespeare. You can see the prose stepping off.

The germinous seeds Hawthorne has dropped in Melville's July soil begin to grow: Bulkington, the secret member of the crew in *Moby-Dick,* is here, hidden in what Melville quotes as Hawthorne's self-portrait—the "seeker," rough-hewn and brawny, of large, warm heart and powerful intellect.

Above all, in the ferment, Shakespeare, the cause. The passages on him—the manner in which he is introduced, the detail with which he is used, the intensity—tell the story of what had happened. Melville had read him again. His copy of THE PLAYS survives. He had bought it in Boston in February, 1849. He described it then to Duyckinck:

> It is an edition in glorious great type, every letter whereof is a soldier, & the top of every 't' like a musket barrel.

I am mad to think how minute a cause has prevented me hitherto from reading Shakespeare. But until now any copy that was come-atable to me happened to be a vile small print unendurable to my eyes which are tender as young sperms.

But chancing to fall in with this glorious edition, I now exult over it, page after page.

The set exists, seven volumes, with passages marked, and comments in Melville's hand. The significant thing is the rough notes for the composition of *Moby-Dick* on the fly-leaf of the last volume. These notes involve Ahab, Pip, Bulkington, Ishmael, and are the key to Melville's intention with these characters. They thus relate not to what we know of the Moby-Dick that Melville had been working on up to July but to *Moby-Dick* as he came to conceive it at this time.

Joined to the passages on Shakespeare in the Mosses piece, the notes in the Shakespeare set verify what *Moby-Dick* proves: Melville and Shakespeare had made a Corinth and out of the burning came *Moby-Dick, bronze*. . . .

A *MOBY-DICK* MANUSCRIPT

It is beautifully right to find what I take to be rough notes for *Moby-Dick* in the Shakespeare set itself. They are written in Melville's hand, in pencil, upon the last fly-leaf of the last volume, the one containing *Lear, Othello* and *Hamlet*. I transcribe them as they stand:

> Ego non baptizo te in nomine Patris et
> Filii et Spiritus Sancti—sed in nomine
> Diaboli.—madness is undefinable—
> It & right reason extremes of one,
> —not the (black art) Goetic but Theurgic magic—
> seeks converse with the Intelligence, Power, the
> Angel.

The Latin is a longer form of what Melville told Hawthorne to be the secret motto of *Moby-Dick*. In the novel Ahab howls it as an inverted benediction upon the harpoon he has tempered in savage blood:

Ego non baptizo te in nomine patris, sed in nomine diaboli.

I do not baptize thee in the name of the father, but in the name of the devil.

The change in the wording from the notes to the novel is of extreme significance. It is not for economy of phrase. The removal of Christ and the Holy Ghost—Filii et Spiritus Sancti—is a mechanical act mirroring the imaginative. Of necessity, from Ahab's world, both Christ and the Holy Ghost are absent. Ahab moves and has his being in a world to which They and what They import are inimical: remember, Ahab fought a deadly scrimmage with a Spaniard before the altar at Santa, and spat into the silver calabash. The conflict in Ahab's world is abrupt, more that between Satan and Jehovah, of the old dispensation than the new. It is the outward symbol of the inner truth that the name of Christ is uttered but once in the book and then it is torn from Starbuck, the only possible man to use it, at a moment of anguish, the night before the fatal third day of the chase.

Ahab is Conjur Man. He invokes his own evil world. He himself uses black magic to achieve his vengeful ends. With the very words "in nomine diaboli" he believes he utters a Spell and performs a Rite of such magic.

The Ahab-world is closer to *Macbeth* than to *Lear*. In it the supernatural is accepted. Fedallah appears as freely as the Weird Sisters. Before Ahab's first entrance he has reached that identification with evil to which Macbeth out of fear evolves within the play itself. The agents of evil give both Ahab and Macbeth a false security through the same device, the unfulfillable prophecy. Ahab's tense and nervous speech is like Macbeth's, rather than Lear's. Both Macbeth and Ahab share a common hell of wicked, sleep-bursting dreams. They both endure the torture of isolation from humanity. The correspondence of these two evil worlds is precise. In either the divine has little place. Melville intended certain exclusions, and Christ and the Holy Ghost were two of them. Ahab, alas, could not even baptize in the name of the Father. He could only do it in the name of the Devil.

That is the Ahab-world, and it is wicked. Melville meant exactly what he wrote to Hawthorne when the book was consummated:

I have written a wicked book, and feel as spotless as the lamb.

Melville's "wicked book" is the drama of Ahab, his hot hate for the White Whale, and his vengeful pursuit of it from the moment the ship plunges like fate into the Atlantic. It is that action, not the complete novel *Moby-Dick*. The *Moby-Dick* universe contains more, something different. Perhaps the difference is the reason why Melville felt "spotless as the lamb." The rough notes in the Shakespeare embrace it.

"Madness is undefinable." Two plays from which the thought could have sprung are in the volume in which it is written down: *Lear* and *Hamlet*. Of the modes of madness in *Lear*—the King's, the Fool's—which is definable? But we need not rest on supposition as to what Melville drew of madness from *Hamlet,* or from *Lear: Moby-Dick* includes both Ahab and Pip. Melville forces his analysis of Ahab's mania to incredible distances, only himself to admit that "Ahab's larger, darker, deeper part remains unhinted." Pip's is a more fathomable idiocy: "his shipmates called him mad." Melville challenges the description, refuses to leave Pip's madness dark and unhinted, declares: "So man's insanity is heaven's sense."

The emphasis in this declaration is the key to resolve apparent difficulties in the last sentence of the notes in the Shakespeare volume:

> It & right reason extremes of one,—not the (black art) Goetic
> but Theurgic magic—seeks converse with the Intelligence,
> Power, the Angel.

I take "it" to refer to the "madness" of the previous sentence. "Right reason," less familiar to the 20th century, meant more to the last, for in the Kant-Coleridge terminology "right reason" described the highest range of the intelligence and stood in contrast to "understanding." Melville had used the phrase in *Mardi.* What he did with it there discloses what meaning it had for him when he used it in these cryptic notes for the composition of *Moby-Dick. Mardi:*

> Right reason, and Alma (Christ), are the same; else Alma, not
> reason, would we reject. The Master's great command is Love;
> and here do all things wise, and all things good, unite. Love is
> all in all. The more we love, the more we know; and so reversed.

Now, returning to the notes, if the phrase "not the (black art) Goetic but Theurgic magic" is recognized as parenthetical, the sentence has some clarity: "madness" and its apparent opposite "right reason" are the two extremes of one way or attempt or urge to reach "the Intelligence, Power, the Angel" or, quite simply, God.

The adjectives of the parenthesis bear this reading out. "Goetic" might seem to derive from Goethe and thus *Faust,* but its source is the Greek "goetos," meaning variously trickster, juggler and, as here, magician. (Plato called literature "Goeteia.") Wherever Melville picked up the word he means it, as he says, for the "black art." "Theurgic," in sharp contrast, is an accurate term for a kind of occult art of the Neoplatonists in which, through self-purification and sacred rites, the aid of the divine was evoked. In thus opposing "Goetic" and "Theurgic" Melville is using a distinction as old as Chaldea between black and white magic, the one of demons, the other of saints and angels, one evil, the other benevolent. For white or

"Theurgic" magic, like "madness" and "right reason," seeks God, while the "black art Goetic" invokes only the devil.

Now go to *Moby-Dick*. In the Ahab-world there is no place for "converse with the Intelligence, Power, the Angel." Ahab cannot seek it, for understood between him and Fedallah is a compact as binding as Faust's with Mephistopheles. Melville's assumption is that though both Ahab and Faust may be seekers after truth, a league with evil closes the door to truth. Ahab's art, so long as his hate survives, is black. He does not seek true converse.

"Madness," on the contrary, does, and Pip is mad, possessed of an insanity which is "heaven's sense." When the little Negro almost drowned, his soul went down to wondrous depths and there he "saw God's foot upon the treadle of the loom, and spoke it." Through that accident Pip, of all the crew, becomes "prelusive of the eternal time" and thus achieves the converse Ahab has denied himself by his blasphemy. The chapter on THE DOUBLOON dramatizes the attempts on the part of the chief active characters to reach truth. In that place Starbuck, in his "mere unaided virtue," is revealed to have no abiding faith: he retreats before "Truth," fearing to lose his "righteousness." . . . Stubb's jollity and Flask's clod-like stupidity blunt the spiritual. . . . The Manxman has mere superstition, Queequeg mere curiosity. . . . Fedallah worships the doubloon evilly. . . . Ahab sees the gold coin solipsistically: "three peaks as proud as Lucifer" and all named "Ahab!" Pip alone, of all, has true prescience: he names the doubloon the "navel" of the ship—"Truth" its life.

"Right reason" is the other way to God. It is the way of man's sanity, the pure forging of his intelligence in the smithy of life. To understand what use Melville made of it in *Moby-Dick* two characters, both inactive to the plot, have to be brought forth.

Bulkington is the man who corresponds to "right reason." Melville describes him once early in the book when he enters the Spouter Inn. "Six feet in height, with noble shoulders, and a chest like a coffer-dam." In the deep shadows of his eyes "floated some reminiscences that did not seem to give him much joy." In the LEE SHORE chapter Bulkington is explicitly excluded from the action of the book, but not before Melville has, in ambiguities, divulged his significance as symbol. Bulkington is Man who, by "deep, earnest thinking" puts out to sea, scorning the land, convinced that "in landlessness alone resides the highest truth, shoreless, indefinite as God."

The rest of the *Pequod*'s voyage Bulkington remains a "sleeping-partner" to the action. He is the secret member of the crew, below deck always, like the music under the earth in *Antony and Cleopatra,* strange. He is the crew's heart, the sign of their paternity, the human thing. And by that human thing alone can they reach their apotheosis.

There remains Ishmael. Melville framed Ahab's action, and the parts Pip, Bulkington and the rest of the crew played in the action, within a narrative told by Ishmael. Too long in criticism of the novel Ishmael has been confused with Herman Melville himself. Ishmael is fictive, imagined, as are Ahab, Pip and Bulkington, not so completely perhaps, for the very reason that he is so like his creator. But he is not his creator only: he is a chorus through whom Ahab's tragedy is seen, by whom what is black and what is white magic is made clear. Like the Catskill eagle Ishmael is able to dive down into the blackest gorges and soar out to the light again.

He is passive and detached, the observer, and thus his separate and dramatic existence is not so easily felt. But unless his choric function is recognized some of the vision of the book is lost. When he alone survived the wreck of the *Pequod,* he remained, after the shroud of the sea rolled on, to tell more than Ahab's wicked story. Ahab's self-created world, in essence privative, a thing of blasphemies and black magic, has its offset. Ahab has to dominate over a world where the humanities may also flower and man (the crew) by Pip's or Bulkington's way reach God. By this use of Ishmael Melville achieved a struggle and a catharsis which he intended, to feel "spotless as the lamb."

Ishmael has that cleansing ubiquity of the chorus in all drama, back to the Greeks. It is interesting that, in the same place where the notes for *Moby-Dick* are written in his Shakespeare, Melville jots down: "Eschylus Tragedies." Ishmael alone hears Father Mapple's sermon out. He alone saw Bulkington, and understood him. It was Ishmael who learned the secrets of Ahab's blasphemies from the prophet of the fog, Elijah. He recognized Pip's God-sight, and moaned for him. He cries forth the glory of the crew's humanity. Ishmael tells *their* story and *their* tragedy as well as Ahab's, and thus creates the *Moby-Dick* universe in which the Ahab-world is, by the necessity of life—or the Declaration of Independence—*included. . . .*

SHAKESPEARE CONCLUDED

Melville was no naïve democrat. He recognized the persistence of the "great man" and faced, in 1850, what we have faced in the 20th century. At the time of the rise of the common man Melville wrote a tragedy out of the rise, and the fall, of uncommon Ahab.

In the old days of the Mediterranean and Europe it was the flaw of a king which brought tragedy to men. A calamity was that which "unwar strook the regnes that been proude." When fate was feudal, and a great man fell, his human property, the people, paid.

A whaleship reminded Melville of two things: (1) democracy had not rid itself of overlords; (2) the common man, however free, leans on a leader, the leader, however dedicated, leans on a straw. He pitched his tragedy right there.

America 1850 was his GIVEN:

"a poor old whale-hunter" the great man;

fate, the chase of the Sperm whale, plot (economics is the administration of scarce resources);

the crew the commons, the Captain over them;

EQUALS:

tragedy.

For a consideration of dominance in man, read by all means the chapter in *Moby-Dick* called THE SPECKSYNDER, concerning emperors and kings, the forms and usages of the sea.

through these forms that certain sultanism of Ahab's brain became incarnate in an irresistible dictatorship.

For be a man's intellectual superiority what it will, it can never assume the practical, available supremacy over other men, without the aid of some sort of external arts and entrenchments, always, in themselves, more or less paltry and base.

Nor will the tragic dramatist who would depict mortal indomitableness in its fullest sweep and direct swing, ever forget a hint, incidentally so important in his art, as the one now alluded to.

More, much more.

Melville saw his creative problem clearly:

He had a prose world, a NEW.
But it was "tragedie," old.
Shakespeare gave him a bag of tricks.
The Q.E.D.: *Moby-Dick.*

The shape of *Moby-Dick,* like the meaning of its action, has roots deep in THE PLAYS. Melville studied Shakespeare's craft. For example, *characterization.* In at least three places Melville analyzes *Hamlet.* There are two in *Pierre*. One enlarges upon the only note he writes in his copy of the play: "the great Montaignism of Hamlet." The third and most interesting passage is in *The Confidence-Man*. There Melville makes a distinction between the making of "odd" and the creation of "original" characters in literature. Of the latter he allows only three: Milton's Satan, Quixote, and Hamlet. The original character is

> like a revolving Drummond light, raying away from itself all round it—everything is lit by it, everything starts up to it (mark how it is with Hamlet).

Melville likens the effect to "that which in Genesis attends upon the beginning of things." In the creation of Ahab Melville made the best use of that lesson he knew how.

Structure, likewise. *Moby-Dick* has a rise and fall like the movement of an Elizabethan tragedy. The first twenty-two chapters, in which Ishmael as chorus narrates the preparations for the voyage, are precedent to the action and prepare for it. Chapter XXIII is an interlude, THE LEE SHORE; Bulkington, because he is "right reason," is excluded from the tragedy. With the next chapter the book's drama begins. The first act ends in the QUARTER-DECK chapter, the first precipitation of action, which brings together for the first time Ahab, the crew, and the purpose of the voyage— the chase of the White Whale. All the descriptions of the characters, all the forebodings, all the hints are brought to their first manifestation.

Another interlude follows: Ishmael expands upon MOBY-DICK and THE WHITENESS OF THE WHALE

Merely to summarize what follows, the book then moves up to the meeting with the *Jeroboam* and her mad prophet Gabriel (chp. LXXI) and, after that, in a third swell, into the visit of Ahab to the *Samuel Enderby* to see her captain who had lost his arm as Ahab his leg to Moby-Dick (chp. C). The pitch of the action is the storm scene, THE CANDLES From that point on Ahab comes to repose, fifth act, in his fate.

In this final movement Moby-Dick appears, for the first time. It is a mistake to think of the Whale as antagonist in the usual dramatic sense. (In democracy the antagonisms are wide.) The demonisms are dispersed, and Moby-Dick but the more assailable mass of them. In fact the actual physical whale finally present in *Moby-Dick* is more comparable to death's function in Elizabethan tragedy: when the white thing is encountered first, he is in no flurry, but quietly gliding through the sea, "a mighty mildness of repose in swiftness."

Obviously *Moby-Dick* is a novel and not a play. It contains creations impossible to any stage—a ship the *Pequod,* whales, Leviathan, the vast sea. In the making of most of his books Melville used similar things. In *Moby-Dick* he integrated them as he never had before nor was to again.

The whaling matter is stowed away as he did not manage the ethnology of *Typee* nor was to, the parables of *The Confidence-Man.* While the book is getting under way—that is, in the first forty-eight chapters—Melville allows only four "scientific" chapters on whaling to appear. Likewise, as the book sweeps to its tragic close in the last thirty chapters, Melville rules out all such exposition. The body of the book supports the bulk of the matter on the Sperm whale—"scientific or poetic." Melville carefully controls these chapters, skillfully breaking them up: the eight different vessels the *Pequod* meets as she moves across the oceans slip in and cut between the considerations of cetology. Actually and deliberately the whaling chapters brake the advance of the plot. Van Wyck Brooks called them "ballast."

Stage directions appear throughout. *Soliloquies,* too. There is a significant use of the special Elizabethan soliloquy to the skull in Ahab's mutterings to the Sperm whale's head in THE SPHINX (chp. LXX). One of the subtlest *supernatural effects,* the "low laugh from the hold" in the QUARTER-DECK scene, echoes Shakespeare's use of the Ghost below ground in *Hamlet.*

Properties are used for precise theater effect. Ahab smashes his quadrant as Richard his mirror. Of them the Doubloon is the most important. Once Ahab has nailed the coin to the mast it becomes FOCUS. The imagery, the thought, the characters, the events precedent and to come, are centered on it. It is there, midstage, Volpone, gold.

Of the soliloquies, Ahab's show the presence of *Elizabethan speech* most. The cadences and acclivities of Melville's prose change. Melville characterized Ahab's language as "nervous, lofty." In the soliloquies it is jagged like that of a Shakespearean hero whose speech like his heart often cracks in the agony of fourth and fifth act.

The long ease and sea swell of Ishmael's narrative prose contrasts this short, rent language of Ahab. The opposition of cadence is part of the counterpoint of the book. It adumbrates the part the two characters play, Ishmael the passive, Ahab the active. More than that, it arises from and returns, contrapunto, to the whole concept of the book revealed by the notes in Melville's copy of Shakespeare—the choric Ishmael can, like the Catskill eagle, find the light, but Ahab, whose only magic is Goetic, remains dark. The contrast in prose repeats the theme of calm and tempest which runs through the novel. Without exception action rises out of calm, whether it is the first chase of a whale, the appearance of the Spirit Spout, the storm, or the final chase of Moby-Dick precipitously following upon the THE SYMPHONY.

As the strongest literary force Shakespeare caused Melville to approach tragedy in terms of the drama. As the strongest social force America caused him to approach tragedy in terms of democracy.

It was not difficult for Melville to reconcile the two. Because of his perception of America: Ahab.

It has to do with size, and how you value it. You can approach BIG America and spread yourself like a pancake, sing her stretch as Whitman did, be puffed up as we are over PRODUCTION. It's easy. THE AMERICAN WAY. Soft. Turns out paper cups, lies flat on the brush. N.G.

Or recognize that our power is simply QUANTITY. Without considering purpose. Easy too. That is, so long as we continue to be INGENIOUS about machines, and have the resources.

Or you can take an attitude, the creative vantage. See her as OBJECT in MOTION, something to be shaped, for use. It involves a first act of physics. You can observe POTENTIAL and VELOCITY separately, have to, to measure THE THING. You get approximate results. They are usable enough if you include the Uncertainty Principle, Heisenberg's law that you learn the speed at the cost of exact knowledge of the energy and the energy at the loss of the exact knowledge of the speed.

Melville did his job. He calculated, and cast Ahab. BIG, first of all. ENERGY, next. PURPOSE: lordship over nature. SPEED: of the brain. DIRECTION: vengeance. COST: the people, the Crew.

Ahab is the FACT, the Crew the IDEA. The Crew is where what America stands for got into Moby-Dick. They're what we imagine democracy to be. They're Melville's addition to tragedy as he took it from Shakespeare. He had to do more with the people than offstage shouts in a Julius Caesar. This was the difference a Declaration of Independence made. In his copy of the play Melville writes the note

Tammany Hall

in heavy strokes beside Casca's description of the Roman rabble before Caesar:

> If the tag-rag people did not clap him and hiss him, according
> as he pleas'd and displeas'd them, as they use to do the players
> in the theatre, I am no true man.

Melville thought he had more searoom to tell the truth. He was writing in a country where an Andrew Jackson could, as he put it, be "hurled higher than a throne." A political system called "democracy" had led men to think they were "free" of aristocracy. The fact of the matter is Melville couldn't help but give the "people" a larger part because in the life around him they played a larger part. He put it this way:

> this august dignity I treat of, is not the dignity of kings and robes, but that abounding dignity which has no robed investiture.

> Thou shalt see it shining in the arm that wields a pick and drives a spike; that democratic dignity which, on all hands, radiates without end from God; Himself! The great God absolute! The center and circumference of all democracy! His omnipresence, our divine equality!

> If, then, to meanest mariners, and renegades and castaways, I shall hereafter ascribe high qualities, though dark; weave round them tragic graces; if even the most mournful, perchance the most abased, among them all, shall at times lift himself to the exalted mounts; if I shall touch that workman's arm with some ethereal light; if I shall spread a rainbow over his disastrous set of sun; then against all mortal critics bear me out in it, thou just Spirit of Equality, which hast spread one royal mantle of humanity over all my kind!

Remember Bulkington.

To MAGNIFY is the mark of *Moby-Dick*. As with workers, castaways, so with the scope and space of the sea, the prose, the Whale, the Ship and, OVER ALL, the Captain. It is the technical act compelled by the American fact. Cubits of tragic stature. Put it this way. Three forces operated to bring about the dimensions of *Moby-Dick:* Melville, a man of MYTH, antemosaic: an experience of SPACE, its power and price, America; and ancient magnitudes of TRAGEDY, Shakespeare.

It is necessary now to consider *Antony and Cleopatra,* the play Melville pencilled most heavily. Rome was the World, and Shakespeare gives his people and the action imperial size. His hero and heroine love as Venus and Mars, as planets might.

> His legs bestrid the ocean; his rear'd arm
> Crested the world.

So Cleopatra dreamed of Antony. Melville marked her words. He marked Antony's joyful greeting to Cleopatra after he has beaten Caesar back to his camp:

> O thou day o' th' world!

And Cleopatra's cry of grief when Antony dies:

> The crown o' th' earth doth melt.

Antony and Cleopatra is an East. It is built as Pyramids were built. There is space here, and objects big enough to contest space. These are men and women who live life large. The problems are the same but they work themselves out on a stage as wide as ocean.

When Enobarbus comments on Antony's flight from Actium in pursuit of Cleopatra, we are precisely within the problems of *Moby-Dick:*

> To be furious
> Is to be frighted out of fear, and in that mood
> The dove will peck the estridge. I see still
> A diminution in our captain's brain
> Restores his heart. When valour preys on reason
> It eats the sword it fights with.

In exactly what way Ahab, furious and without fear, retained the instrument of his reason as a lance to fight the White Whale is a central concern of Melville's in *Moby-Dick.* In his Captain there was a diminution in his heart.

From whaling, which America had made distinctly a part of her industrial empire, he took this "poor old whale-hunter," as he called him, this man of "Nantucket grimness and shagginess." Out of such stuff he had to make his tragic hero, his original. He faced his difficulties. He knew he was denied "the outward majestical trappings and housings" that Shakespeare had for his Antony, his Lear and his Macbeth. Melville wrote:

> Oh, Ahab! what shall be grand in thee, must needs be plucked
> at from the skies, and dived for in the deep, and featured in the
> unbodied air!

He made him "a khan of the plank, and a king of the sea, and a great lord of leviathans." For the American has the Roman feeling about the world. It is his, to dispose of. He strides it, with possession of it. His property.

Has he not conquered it with his machines? He bends its resources to his will. The pax of legions? the Americanization of the world. Who else is lord?

Melville isolates Ahab in "a Grand-Lama-like exclusiveness." He is captain of the *Pequod* because of "that certain sultanism of his brain." He is proud and morbid, willful, vengeful. He wears a "hollow crown," not Richard's. It is the Iron Crown of Lombardy which Napoleon wore. Its jagged edge, formed from a nail of the Crucifixion, galls him. He worships fire and swears to strike the sun.

OVER ALL, hate—huge and fixed upon the imperceptible. Not man but all the hidden forces that terrorize man is assailed by the American Timon. That HATE, extra-human, involves his Crew, and Moby-Dick drags them to their death as well as Ahab to his, a collapse of a hero through solipsism which brings down a world.

At the end of the book, in the heart of the White Whale's destruction, the Crew and Pip and Bulkington and Ahab lie down together.

All scatt'red in the bottom of the sea.

"In Nomine Diaboli": Moby-Dick

Henry A. Murray

Some writers have said that there is nothing to interpret [in *Moby-Dick*]: it is a plain sea story marred here and there by irrelevant ruminations. But I shall not cite the abundant proof for the now generally accepted proposition that in *Moby-Dick* Melville "meant" something—something, I should add, which he considered "terrifically true" but which, in the world's judgment, was so harmful "that it were all but madness for any good man, in his own proper character, to utter or even hint of." What seems decisive here is the passage in Melville's celebrated letter to Hawthorne: "A sense of unspeakable security is in me this moment, on account of your having understood the book." From this we can conclude that there *are* meanings to be understood in *Moby-Dick*, and also—may we say for our own encouragement?— that Melville's ghost will feel secure forever if modern critics can find them and, since Hawthorne remained silent, set them forth in print. Here it might be well to remind ourselves of a crucial statement which follows the just quoted passage from Melville's letter: "I have written a wicked book." The implication is clear: all interpretations which fail to show that *Moby-Dick* is, in some sense, wicked have missed the author's avowed intention.

A few critics have scouted all attempts to fish Melville's own meaning out of *The Whale*, on the ground that an interpretation of a work of art so vast and so complex is bound to be composed in large measure of projections from the mind of the interpreter. It must be granted that preposterous projections often do occur in the course of such an effort. But these are not

From *New England Quarterly* 24 (December 1951). © 1951 by *New England Quarterly*. Originally entitled "In Nomine Diaboli."

inevitable. Self-knowledge and discipline may reduce projections to a minimum. Anyhow, in the case of *Moby-Dick*, the facts do not sustain the proposition that a critic can see nothing in this book but his own reflected image. The interpretations which have been published over the last thirty years exhibit an unmistakable trend toward consensus in respect to the drama as a whole as well as to many of its subordinate parts. Moreover, so far as I can judge, the critics who, with hints from their predecessors, applied their intuitions most recently to the exegesis of *The Whale* can be said to have arrived, if taken together, at Melville's essential meaning. Since one or another of these authors has deftly said what I clumsily thought, my prejudices are strongly in favor of their conclusions, and I am wholehearted in applauding them—Newton Arvin's most especially—despite their having left me with nothing fresh to say. Since this is how things stand, my version of the main theme of *Moby-Dick* can be presented in a briefer form, and limited to two hypotheses.

The first of them is this: Captain Ahab is an embodiment of that fallen angel or demi-god who in Christendom was variously named Lucifer, Devil, Adversary, Satan. The Church Fathers would have called Captain Ahab "Antichrist" because he was not Satan himself, but a human creature possessed of all Satan's pride and energy, "summing up within himself," as Irenaeus said, "the apostasy of the devil."

That it was Melville's intention to beget Ahab in Satan's image can hardly be doubted. He told Hawthorne that his book had been broiled in hell-fire and secretly baptized not in the name of God but in the name of the Devil. He named his tragic hero after the Old Testament ruler who "did more to provoke the Lord God of Israel to anger than all the Kings of Israel that were before him." King Ahab's accuser, the prophet Elijah, is also resurrected to play his original role, though very briefly, in Melville's testament. We are told that Captain Ahab is an "ungodly, god-like" man who is spiritually outside Christendom. He is a well of blasphemy and defiance, of scorn and mockery for the gods—"cricket-players and pugilists" in his eyes. Rumor has it that he once spat in the holy goblet on the altar of the Catholic Church at Santa. "I never saw him kneel," says Stubb. He is associated in the text with scores of references to the Devil. He is an "anaconda of an old man." His self-assertive sadism is the linked antithesis of the masochistic submission preached by Father Mapple.

Captain Ahab-Lucifer is also related to a sun-god, like Christ, but in reverse. Instead of being light leaping out of darkness, he is "darkness leaping out of light." The *Pequod* sails on Christmas Day. *This* new year's sun will be the god of Wrath rather than the god of Love. Ahab does not emerge from his subteranean abode until his ship is "rolling through the bright Quito spring" (Eastertide, symbolically, when the all-fertilizing sun-god is resurrected). The frenzied ceremony in which Ahab's followers are sworn to the pursuit of the White Whale—"Commend the murderous chalices!"—is suggestive of the Black Mass; the lurid operations at the tryworks is a scene out of Hell.

There is some evidence that Melville was rereading *Paradise Lost* in the summer of 1850, shortly after, let us guess, he got the idea of transforming the captain of his whale-ship into the first of all cardinal sinners who fell by pride. Anyhow, Melville's Satan is the spitting image of Milton's hero, but portrayed with deeper and subtler psychological insight, and placed where he belongs, in the heart of an enraged man.

Melville may have been persuaded by Goethe's Mephistopheles, or even by some of Hawthorne's bloodless abstracts of humanity, to add Fedallah to his cast of characters. Evidently he wanted to make certain that no reader would fail to recognize that Ahab had been possessed by, or had sold his soul to the Devil. Personally, I think Fedallah's role is superfluous, and I regret that Melville made room for him and his unbelievable boat-crew on the ship *Pequod*. Still, he is not wholly without interest. He rep-resents the cool, heartless, cunning, calculating, intellectual Devil of the medieval myth-makers, in contrast to the stricken, passionate, indignant, and often eloquent rebel angel of *Paradise Lost*, whose role is played by Ahab.

The Arabic name "Fedallah" suggests "dev(il) Allah," that is, the Mo-hammedans' god as he appeared in the mind's eye of a Crusader. But we are told that Fedallah is a Parsee—a Persian fire-worshiper, or Zoroastrian, who lives in India. Thus, Ahab, named after the Semitic apostate who was converted to the orgiastic cult of Baal, or Bel, originally a Babylonian fertility god, has formed a compact with a Zoroastrian whose name reminds us of still another Oriental religion. In addition, Captain Ahab's whaleboat is manned by a crew of unregenerated infidels, as defined by orthodox Christianity; and each of his three harpooners, Queequeg, Tashtego, and Daggoo, is a member of a race which believed in other gods than the one god of the Hebraic-Christian Bible.

Speaking roughly, it might be said that Captain Ahab, incarnation of the Adversary and master of the ship *Pequod* (named after the aggressive Indian tribe that was exterminated by the Puritans of New England), has summoned the various religions of the East to combat the one dominant religion of the West. Or, in other terms, that he and his followers, Starbuck excepted, represent the horde of primitive drives, values, beliefs, and practices which 'the Hebraic-Christian religionists rejected and excluded, and by threats, punishments, and inquisitions forced into the unconscious mind of Western man.

Stated in psychological concepts, Ahab is captain of the culturally repressed dispositions of human nature, that part of personality which psychoanalysts have termed the "Id." If this is true, his opponent, the White Whale, can be none other than the internal institution which is responsible for these repressions, namely the Freudian Superego. This, then, is my second hypothesis; Moby-Dick is a veritable spouting, breaching, sounding whale, a whale who, because of his whiteness, his mighty bulk and beauty, and because of one instinctive act that happened to dismember his assailant, has received the projection of Captain Ahab's Presbyterian conscience, and so may be said to embody the Old Testament Calvinistic conception of an affrighting Deity and his strict commandments, the derivative puritan ethic of nineteenth-century America and the society that defended this ethic. Also, and most specifically, he symbolizes the zealous parents whose righteous sermonizings and corrections drove the prohibitions in so hard that a serious young man could hardly reach outside the barrier, except possibly far away among some tolerant, gracious Polynesian peoples. The emphasis should be placed on that unconscious (and hence inscrutable) wall of inhibition which imprisoned the Puritan's thrusting passions. "How can the prisoner reach outside," cries Ahab, "except by thrusting through the wall? To me, the white whale is that wall, shoved near to me . . . I see in him outrageous strength, with an inscrutable malice sinewing it." As a symbol of a sounding, breaching, white-dark, unconquerable New England conscience what could be better than a sounding, breaching, white-dark, unconquerable sperm whale?

Who is the psychoanalyst who could resist the immediate inference that the imago of the mother as well as the imago of the father is contained in the Whale? In the present case there happens to be a host of biographical facts and written passages which support this proposition. Luckily, I need not review them, because Mr. Arvin and others have come to the same conclusion. I shall confine myself to one reference. It exhibits Melville's keen and sympathetic insight into the cultural determinants of his mother's prohibiting dispositions. In *Pierre*, it is the "high-up, and towering and all-forbidding . . . edifice of his mother's immense pride . . . her pride of birth . . . her pride of purity," that is the "wall shoved near," the wall that stands between the hero and the realization of his heart's resolve. But instead of expending the fury of frustration upon his mother, he directs it at Fate, or, more specifically, at his mother's God and the society that shaped her. For he sees "that not his mother has made his mother; but the Infinite Haughtiness had first fashioned her; and then the haughty world had further molded her; nor had a haughty Ritual omitted to finish her."

Given this penetrating apprehension, we are in a position to say that Melville's target in *Moby-Dick* was the upper-middle class culture of his time. It was *this* culture which was defended with righteous indignation by what he was apt to call "the world" or "the public," and Melville had very little respect for "the world" or "the public." The "public," or men operating as a social system, was something quite distinct from "the people." In *White-Jacket* he wrote: "The public and the people! . . . let us hate the one, and cleave to the other." "The public is a monster," says Lemsford. Still earlier Melville had said: "I fight against the armed and crested lies of Mardi (the world)." "Mardi is a monster whose eyes are fixed in its head, like a whale." Many other writers have used similar imagery. Sir Thomas Browne referred to the multitude as "that numerous piece of monstrosity." Keats spoke of "the dragon world." But closest of all was Hobbes: "By art is created that great Leviathan, called a commonwealth or state." It is in the laws of this Leviathan, Hobbes made clear, that the sources of right and wrong reside. To summarize: the giant mass of Melville's whale is the same as Melville's man-of-war world, the *Neversink*, in *White-Jacket*, which in turn is an epitome of Melville's Mardi. The Whale's white forehead and hump should be reserved for the world's heavenly King.

That God is incarnate in the Whale has been perceived by Geoffrey Stone, and, as far as I know, by every other Catholic critic of Melville's work, as well as by several Protestant critics. In fact, Richard Chase has marshaled so fair a portion of the large bulk of evidence on this point that any more from me would be superfluous. Of course, what Ahab projects into the Whale is not the image of a loving Father, but the God of the Old Dispensation, the God who brought Jeremiah into darkness, hedged him about, and made his path crooked; the God adopted by the fire-and-brimstone Puritans, who said: "With fury poured out I will rule over you." "The sword without and the terror within, shall destroy both the young man and the virgin." "I will also send the teeth of beasts upon them." "I will heap mischiefs upon them." "To me belongeth vengeance and recompense."

Since the society's vision of deity, and the society's morality, and the parents and ministers who implant these conceptions, are represented in a fully socialized personality by an establishment that is called the Superego—conscience as Freud defined it—and since Ahab has been proclaimed the "Captain of the Id," the simplest psychological formula for Melville's dramatic epic is this: an insurgent Id in mortal conflict with an oppressive cultural Superego. Starbuck, the first mate, stands for the rational realistic Ego, which is overpowered by the fanatical compulsiveness of the Id and dispossessed of its normal regulating functions.

If this is approximately correct, it appears that while writing his greatest work Melville abandoned his detached position in the Ego from time to time, hailed "the realm of shades," as his hero Taji had, and, through the mediumship of Ahab, "burst his hot heart's shell" upon the sacrosanct Almighty and the sacrosanct sentiments of Christendom. Since in the world's judgment, in 1851, nothing could be more reproachable than this, it would be unjust, if not treacherous, of us to reason *Moby-Dick* into some comforting morality play for which no boldness was required. This would be depriving Melville of the ground he gained for self-respect by having dared to abide by his own subjective truth and write a "wicked book," the kind of book that Pierre's publishers, Steel, Flint, and Asbestos, would have called "a blasphemous rhapsody filched from the vile Atheists, Lucian and Voltaire."

Some may wonder how it was that Melville, a fundamentally good, affectionate, noble, idealistic, and reverential man, should have felt impelled to write a wicked book. Why did he aggress so furiously against Western orthodoxy, as furiously as Byron and Shelley, or any Satanic writer who preceded him, as furiously as Nietzsche or the most radical of his successors in our day?

In *Civilization and Its Discontents* Freud, out of the ripeness of his full experience, wrote that when one finds deepseated aggression—and by this he meant aggression of the sort that Melville voiced—one can safely attribute it to the frustration of Eros. In my opinion this generalization does not hold for all men of all cultures of all times, but the probability of its being valid is extremely high in the case of an earnest, moralistic, nineteenth-century American, a Presbyterian to boot, whose anger is born of suffering—especially if this man spent an impressionable year of his life in Polynesia and returned to marry the very proper little daughter of the chief justice of Massachusetts, and if, in addition, he is a profoundly creative man in whose androgynic personality masculine and feminine components are integrally blended.

If it were concerned with *Moby-Dick*, the book, rather than with its author, I would call *this* my third hypothesis: Ahab-Melville's aggression was directed against the object that once harmed Eros with apparent malice and was still thwarting it with presentiments of further retaliations. The correctness of this inference is indicated by the nature of the injury—a symbolic emasculation—that excited Ahab's ire. Initially, this threatening object was, in all likelihood, the father; later, possibly, the mother. But, as Melville plainly saw, both his parents had been fashioned by the Hebraic-Christian, American Calvinistic tradition, the tradition which conceived of a deity in whose eyes Eros was depravity. It was the first Biblical myth-makers who dismissed from heaven and from earth the Great Goddess of the Oriental and primitive religions, and so rejected the feminine principle as a spiritual force. Ahab, protagonist of those rejected religions, in addressing heaven's fire and lightning, what he calls "the personified impersonal," cries: "but thou art my fiery father; my sweet mother I know not. Oh, cruel! What hast thou done with her?" He calls this god a foundling, a "hermit immemorial," who does not know his own origin. Again, it was the Hebraic authors, sustained later by the Church Fathers, who propagated the legend that a woman was the cause of Adam's exile from Paradise, and that the original sin was concupiscence. Melville says that Ahab, spokesman of all exiled princes, "piled upon the whale's white hump the sum of all the general rage and hate felt by his whole race from Adam down." Remember also that it was the lure of Jezebel that drew King Ahab of Israel outside the orthodoxy of his religion and persuaded him to worship the Phoenician Astarte, goddess of love and fruitful increase. "Jezebel" was the worst tongue-lash a puritan could give a woman. She was sex, and sex was Sin, spelled with a capital. It was the church periodicals of Melville's day that denounced *Typee*, called the author a sensualist, and influenced the publishers to delete suggestive passages from the second edition. It was this long heritage of aversion and animosity, so accentuated in this country, which banned sex relations as a topic of discourse and condemned divorce as an unpardonable offense. All this has been changed, for better and for worse, by the moral revolutionaries of our own time who, feeling as Melville felt but finding the currents of sentiment less strongly opposite, spoke out, and with their wit, indignation, and logic, reinforced by the findings of psychoanalysis, disgraced the stern-faced idols of their forebears. One result is this: today an incompatible marriage is not a prisonhouse, as it was for Melville, "with wall shoved near."

In *Pierre* Melville confessed his own faith when he said that Eros is god of all, and Love "the loftiest religion on this earth." To the romantic Pierre the image of Isabel was "a silent and tyrannical call, challenging him in his deepest moral being, and summoning Truth, Love, Pity, Conscience to the stand." Here he seems to have had in mind the redeeming and inspiriting Eros of courtly love, a heresy which the medieval church had done its utmost to stamp out. *This*, he felt convinced, was *his* "path to

God," although in the way of it he saw with horror the implacable conscience and worldly valuations of his revered mother.

If this line of reasoning is as close as I think it is to the known facts, then Melville, in the person of Ahab, assailed Calvinism in the Whale because it blocked the advance of a conscience beneficent to evolutionary love. And so, weighed in the scales of its creator, *Moby-Dick* is not a wicked book but a *good* book, and after finishing it Melville had full reason to feel, as he confessed, "spotless as the lamb."

But then, seen from another point, *Moby-Dick* might be judged a wicked book, not because its hero condemns an entrenched tradition, but because he is completely committed to destruction. Although Captain Ahab manifests the basic stubborn virtues of the arch-protestant and the rugged individualist carried to their limits, *this* god-defier is no Prometheus, since all thought of benefiting humanity is foreign to him. His purpose is not to make the Pacific safe for whaling, nor, when blasting at the moral order, does he have in mind a more heartening vision for the future. The religion of Eros which might once have been the secret determinant of Ahab's undertaking is never mentioned. At one critical point in *Pierre* the hero-author, favored by a flash of light, exclaims, "I will gospelize the world anew"; but he never does. Out of light comes darkness: the temper of Pierre's book is no different from the temper of *Moby-Dick*. The truth is that Ahab is motivated by his private need to avenge a private insult. His governing philosophy is that of nihilism, the doctrine that the existing system must be shattered. Nihilism springs up when the imagination fails to provide the redeeming solution of an unbearable dilemma, when "the creative response," as Toynbee would say, is not forthcoming, and a man reacts out of a hot heart—"to the dogs with the head"—and swings to an instinct, "the same that prompts even a worm to turn under the heel." This is what White-Jacket did when arraigned at the mast, and what Pierre did when fortune deserted him, and what Billy Budd did when confronted by his accuser. "Nature has not implanted any power in man," said Melville,

> that was not meant to be exercised at times, though too often our powers have been abused. The privilege, inborn, and in-alienable, that every man has, of dying himself and inflicting death upon another, was not given to us without a purpose. These are the last resources of an insulted and unendurable existence.

If we grant that Ahab is a wicked man, what does this prove? It proves that *Moby-Dick* is a *good* book, a parable in epic form, because Melville makes a great spectacle of Ahab's wickedness and shows through the course of the narrative how much wickedness will drive a man on iron rails to an appointed nemesis. Melville adhered to the classic formula for tragedies. He could feel "spotless as the lamb," because he had seen to it that the huge threat to the social system immanent in Ahab's two cardinal defects—egotistic self-inflation and unleashed wrath—was, at the end, fatefully exterminated, "and the great shroud of the sea rolled on as it rolled five thousand years ago." The reader has had his catharsis, equilibrium has been restored, sanity is vindicated.

This is true, but is it the whole truth? In point of fact, while writing *Moby-Dick* did Melville maintain aesthetic distance, keeping his own feelings in abeyance? Do we not hear Ahab saying things that the later Pierre will say and that Melville says less vehemently in his own person? Does not the author show marked partiality for the "mighty pageant creature" of his invention, put in *his* mouth the finest, boldest language? Also, have not many interpreters been so influenced by the abused Ahab that they saw nothing in his opponent but the source of all malicious agencies, the very Devil? As Lewis Mumford has said so eloquently, Ahab is at heart a noble being whose tragic wrong is that of battling against evil with "power instead of love," and so becoming "the image of the thing he hates." With this impression imbedded in our minds, how can we come out with any moral except this: evil wins. We admit that Ahab's wickedness has been canceled. But what survives? It is the much more formidable, compacted wickedness of the group that survives, the world that is "saturated and soaking with lies," and its man-of-war God, who is hardly more admirable than a primitive totem beast, some oral-aggressive, child-devouring Cronos of the sea. Is this an idea that a man of good will can rest with?

Rest with? Certainly not. Melville's clear intention was to bring not rest, but *unrest* to intrepid minds. All gentle people were warned away from his book "on risk of a lumbago or sciatica." "A polar wind blows through it," he announced. He had not written to soothe, but to kindle, to make men leap from their seats, as Whitman would say, and fight for their lives. Was it the poet's function to buttress the battlements of complacency, to give comfort to the enemy? There is little doubt about the nature of the enemy in Melville's day. It was the dominant ideology, that peculiar compound of puritanism and materialism, of rationalism and commercialism, of shallow, blatant optimism and technology, which proved so crushing to creative evolutions in religion, art, and life. In such circumstances every "true poet," as Blake said, "is of the Devil's party," whether he knows it or not. Surveying the last hundred and fifty years, how many exceptions to this statement can we find? Melville, anyhow, knew that *he* belonged to the party, and while writing *Moby-Dick* so gloried in his membership that he baptized his work *In Nomine Diaboli*. It was precisely under these auspices that he created his solitary masterpiece, a construction of the same high order as the Constitution of the United States and the scientific treatises of Willard Gibbs, though huge and wild and unruly as the Grand Canyon. And it is for this marvel chiefly that he resides in our hearts now among the greatest in "that small but high-hushed world" of bestowing geniuses.

The drama is finished. What of its author?

Moby-Dick may be taken as a comment on the strategic crisis of Melville's allegorical life. In portraying the consequences of Ahab's last suicidal lunge, the hero's umbilical fixation to the Whale and his death by strangling, the author signalized not only his permanent attachment to the imago of the mother, but the submission he had foreseen to the binding power of the parental conscience, the Superego of middle-class America. Measured against the standards of *his* day, then, Melville must be accounted a *good* man.

But does this entitle him to a place on the side of the angels? He abdicated to the conscience he condemned, and his ship *Pequod*, in sinking, carried down with it the conscience he aspired to, represented by the sky-hawk, the bird of heaven. With his ideal drowned, life from then on was load, and time stood still. All he had denied to love he gave, throughout a martyrdom of forty years, to death.

But "hark ye yet again—the little lower layer." Melville's capitulation in the face of overwhelming odds was limited to the sphere of action. His embattled soul refused surrender and lived on, breathing back defiance, disputing "to the last gasp" of his "earthquake life" the sovereignty of that inscrutable authority in him. As he wrote in *Pierre*, unless the enthusiast "can find the talismanic secret, to reconcile this world with his own soul, then there is no peace for him, no slightest truce for him in this life." Years later we find him holding the same ground. "Terrible is earth" was his conclusion, but despite all, "no retreat through me." By this stand he bequeathed to us the unsolved problem of the talismanic secret.

Only at the very last, instinct spent, earthquake over, did he fall back to a position close to Christian resignation. In his Being, was not this man "a wonder, a grandeur, and a woe"?

Herman Melville:
Chasing the Whale

David Simpson

> *Nor has Nature been all over ransacked by our progenitors, so that no new charms and mysteries remain for this latter generation to find. Far from it. The trillionth part has not yet been said; and all that has been said, but multiplies the avenues to what remains to be said.*
>
> MELVILLE, *The Literary World*, August 1850

> *We remove mountains, and make seas our smooth highway; nothing can resist us. We war with rude Nature, and, by our resistless engines, come off always victorious, and loaded with spoils.*
>
> CARLYLE, *Signs of the Times*, 1829

Dickens may be described as the analyst of fetishism in the city. He reports on a world of reified imaginations, a whole dismembered into parts seemingly incapable of further restoration. There are exemplary, passionate intelligences to be found, but their eventual success, when it occurs, is more a result of fictional privilege than probability. The Dickens world is a jumble of parts and attributes of exactly the sort foreseen by the earlier theorists of the consequences of divided labor and its influences on mind and society.

Melville and Conrad . . . may be thought of correspondingly as the analysts of fetishism on the high seas and in far-off places. They describe the exportation of the values and customs of that same social configuration so critically addressed by Dickens. It is the imaginations and creative powers of the exporters which are already predetermined by the patterns of seeing and believing which they carry within them, and which are reimposed upon the more innocent—or at least different—world.

From *Fetishism and Imagination: Dickens, Melville, Conrad.* © 1982 by David Simpson. The Johns Hopkins University Press, 1982.

Melville, in the epigraph to this chapter, speaks of the New World—in particular, as it happens, of Vermont, and of the prospects open to the American writer. What makes *Moby-Dick* a book arguably paradoxical in its message is exactly this New World faith in an environment yet unspoiled, and perhaps vast enough to remain forever unspoilable. The white whale is never caught, and thus the energies that go into pursuing him can be at least partly redeemed, if only by complexity, as being somewhere between positive and negative, demonic and creative. The figures of power and conquest are never final: the world fights back, and its horizons recede. The depths of the Pacific may provide the image of infinity which its eastern shores no longer fulfil with conviction.

Carlyle, conversely, speaks from the Old World, the world that Dickens was about to write. These "spoils" too are ambiguous, but the ambiguity does not force us into contradictory positions. They are riches and rewards, and also acts of transgression, spoilings. The one sense taints the other, and suggests that the gains are ill-gotten, bought at the price of criminal interference. Here there is no sense of charm or mystery; here, "nothing can resist us."

Somewhere between these two positions I shall be suggesting [elsewhere] a reading of Conrad, one verging (by fact of residence, perhaps, or time) towards the Old World verdict, with only Marlow and others tugging us back to a world of positive images and an imaginative proliferation of generous principles.

But Conrad and Melville, though coming from different worlds, do have things in common. They both show, as I have said, the idols of the market being carried forth to the societies from whom the very vocabulary of fetishism and idolatry had in the first place been at least partly derived. Such idols have, needless to say, become much more destructive and pervasive than they had ever been in primitive societies. They are no longer as open to idiosyncratic manipulation, to be used or ignored at whim and destroyed if found to be inefficient. They have become solidified, more outwardly fixed and more inwardly infectious, governing now the unconscious processes of the human imagination at the very deepest levels.

In *Typee* Melville makes much play upon the effects of a tailorized invasion on the islanders of the South Seas. He tells the tale of a missionary's wife who inspired nothing less than "idolatry" until the natives realized that she was a mere woman. At this point she was "stripped of her garments, and given to understand that she could no longer carry on her deceits with impunity" (ch. 1). In the absurd trappings of the French admiral, Melville sees "the result of long centuries of progressive civilization and refinement, which have gradually converted the mere creature into the semblance of all that is elevated and grand" (ch. 4). *Typee* conversely has no money and no artifice. In a voice echoing that found in Rousseau and other eighteenth-century writers, Melville compares the islanders' nakedness with the habits of his own civilization: "Stripped of the cunning artifices of the tailor, and standing forth in the garb of Eden,—what a sorry set of round-shouldered, spindle-shanked, crane-necked varlets would civilized men appear! Stuffed calves, padded breasts, and scientifically cut pantaloons would then avail them nothing, and the effect would be truly deplorable" (ch. 25). *Typee* is eloquent on the way in which insidious forms of civilized fetishism are replacing the primitive flexibilities of paradisal life. As a result of encouraging mindless vanity and the worship of ornament among the locals, and setting up a money system to fuel them, the civilized nations are introducing a mirror image of their own social divisions:

> The chiefs swagger about in gold lace and broadcloth, while the great mass of the common people are nearly as primitive in their appearance as in the days of Cook. In the progress of events at these islands, the two classes are receding from each other: the chiefs are daily becoming more luxurious and extravagant in their style of living, and the common people more and more destitute of the necessaries and decencies of life. But the end to which both will arrive at last will be the same: the one are fast destroying themselves by sensual indulgences, and the other are fast *being* destroyed by a complication of disorders, and the want of wholesome food. The resources of the domineering chiefs are wrung from the starving serfs, and every additional bauble with which they bedeck themselves is purchased by the sufferings of their bondsmen; so that the measure of gew-gaw refinement attained by the chiefs is only an index to the actual state of degradation in which the greater portion of the population lie grovelling.
>
> (ch. 26)

But at the same time as all this is acccurately enough moralized by the narrator, in the tradition of so many eighteenth-century writers who had pointed out the mechanisms and dangers of a 'refined' society, there is yet a significant taint of self-implication in his account. Exposed to an alternative culture, he certainly does not go in for the burning of idols, as Crusoe did.

But he does partake of another version of the Puritan inheritance. Besides being a prisoner in the valley (the natives rightly fearing the incursion of more of his kind) he also seems spontaneously dissatisfied: "I can scarcely understand how it was that, in the midst of so many consolatory circumstances, my mind should still have been consumed by the most dismal forebodings, and have remained a prey to the profoundest melancholy" (ch. 16). Though he can see the case for preferring Typee over what he has been born into, 'paradise' is yet dissatisfying. Not being middle ground between hell and heaven, there is nothing for the strenuous consciousness to *do*; play and pleasure themselves become stale for lack of contrast. As, in Dickens, we may infer that the child with no father faces problems just as serious as the child crippled by the imposition of monolithic authority; or, in Hegel, that the paradigm demanded by Hebrew theology is unworkable in its insistence on a totality that is everything and therefore nothing; so, here, the civilized mind becomes frustrated for lack of a focus, an 'other' through which it may anxiously identify itself through reflection. Because he is not to be allowed to escape, he is constantly watched: "not for one single moment that I can recall to mind was I ever permitted to be alone" (ch. 17). If isolation and alienation are the curses incumbent upon man after the Fall, and companionship conversely a prelapsarian ideal, nevertheless that ideal can become unbearable, as it does here, for lack of alternatives. It would be too weighty a reading to suggest that the narrator is passionate in his pursuit of the alienation to which his social and theological training have already habituated him, but we are at least to register the presence of a compulsion that reappears much magnified in *Moby-Dick*.

For the moment, however, I wish to explore another pattern in *Moby-Dick*. For Melville and Conrad also share, being seamen both, an interest in the symptoms and effects of the autonomous male imagination. In the world they write about, male energies are the determining forces, and male figures their images and signs of exchange. Melville hardly writes about women at all, and in Conrad's novels of the colonial experience . . . women typically remain tragically unfulfilled, prophetic of an emotional and social order that has no place in the world already figured. The analysis of the figurative mode that is to be accounted for in Melville and Conrad seems to insist more firmly than ever on the forms of the male psyche as the essential components of the available reality. Fetishism and idolatry, worship of things and of fixed images of the human in their various combinations, seem again to emerge more forcefully than before as founded in the subjective aspirations implicated in phallicism and narcissism. The cycle of desire can now be located, in Melville particularly, as part of a psychology belonging to the male subject and its search for a (specifically) sexual identity, which now becomes both the source and the reference of the fetishistic operation.

Phallicism, defined in terms of its 'rhetorical' characteristics, is a metonymic activity that seeks to persuade its user and his audience that it is in fact synecdochic. The phallus is *not* the penis, but seeks to confirm that it is. It is therefore a detached emblem that must always signal a lack, or a sense of incompletion, and concentration upon it sets in motion a quest that is by definition impossible to fulfil. As a representation it is always alien, never properly open to conversion into the body-part it seeks to image forth. To attempt to accomplish this conversion, by chasing the whale, is to set going a process that can only end in death, unless there is a genuine reeducation of the content and aspiration of consciousness. Further, the mechanisms of the search are shown to contain within them the sources of the compulsions for commerce and colonial expansion, which themselves now become imaginative activities. Mind and matter, the realm of ideal aspirations and the lust for profit, are now inextricably interdetermining, each of the other.

Phallicism, as I have said, is entirely an activity of *representation*; it can never have any place in a direct discourse. Indeed it may be that the very idea of a direct discourse about sexuality and the sexual identity (one which is not, that is to say, performance) is a contradiction in terms. Perhaps any theory of sexual relation and exchange must by definition prescribe its own indirection and fail to encompass the limits of its own deviations, or wanderings. I shall try to show that phallicism, at whatever level of conscious or unconscious decision, is central to the treatment of figures and images, most explicitly in Melville's *Moby-Dick*, but also in Conrad's novels of the colonial experience [elsewhere], where it tends to appear more elliptically.

Phallicism was, in fact, central to the theory of fetishism from its early stages. Dulaure devoted his entire second volume to the subject, deriving its incidence from an original worship of the bull and the he-goat, this giving rise to a spate of derived images of sexual prowess (tree trunks and so forth), including the male organ. From thence, attention passed from part to whole, to the whole human form. Phallicism thus becomes the origin of idolatry, and as such is an original component of all forms of humanized religion. Payne Knight's *An Inquiry into the Symbolical Language of Ancient Art and Mythology* (London, 1818) had also placed strong emphasis on the priapic, and this work remained one of the 'unofficial' source books for the theory of fetishism as it developed through the nineteenth century. For Payne Knight, the universality of priapic images was "acknowledged to the latest periods of heathenism," and he goes so far as to suggest that the "spires and pinnacles, with which our old churches are decorated, came from these ancient symbols." Further, Meiners's *Geschichte der Religionen* has a whole section on phallicism.

Looking back to the incidents from *Robinson Crusoe* and *Typee* discussed [elsewhere], it will be remembered that the idols therein described had implicit if not overt phallic characteristics. James King, the author of the last volume of Cook's *Voyage*, had also remarked that some of the islanders "give a place in their houses to many ludicrous and some obscene idols, like the Priapus of the ancients." In the researches of nineteenth-century anthropologists into the subject of fetishism, it is noticeable that the unabashed discussions of phallicism offered by the earlier theorists begin to disappear or undergo tactful transformations. James Fergusson's *Tree and Serpent Worship* (1868) speaks darkly of certain "unhallowed rites," but says nothing explicit about phallicism. M'Lennan's important articles, which came a year later, move the focus of scientific interest towards totemism and away from fetishism in its looser and broader definitions. Totemism is "fetishism *plus* certain peculiarities"—specificity to a tribe, matrilineal inheritance, and relation to marriage laws. This totemism, whatever origins it might be thought to have in phallicism (the most famous instance of the totem is the pole), becomes with M'Lennan a tool in the organization of primitive societies along rational lines.

For the anthropologist, description of functions and effects replaces (for the most part) speculation about origins. This is the tradition that Frazer inherits, though he does, notably, address himself to origins in speculating that totemism began out of "an ignorance of the part played by the male in the Generation of offspring" (*Totemism and Exogamy*). The woman consequently identifies the moment of conception with the first stirrings in the womb, and associates this with whatever is near her at the time, which then becomes a totem. This is quite close to the origin John Atkins had suggested for fetishism (*Voyage*). It is, in one way, the obverse of phallicism, in which a clear *consciousness* of the power of the generative organ is what inspires the worship of images related to it. Perhaps Frazer's theory partakes of something like a 'reflected' innocence, something the Victorians might have liked to believe in as typical of undeveloped humanity. The contrast of this origin model with that of phallicism is interesting in that the two taken together seem to reflect something close to the extreme polarity that characterizes the representations of males in Dickens's novels. Those who are demonic and aggressive may be thought of as analogous to phallus-worshippers, committed to forceful images of themselves. Conversely, the weak and listless compare with those totemists who have no awareness of any potential sexual energy in themselves, who have abdicated any control over procreation. There is nothing redeeming in the contrast, of course, since both extremes are forms of impotence.

Literature, perhaps, could afford to be more explicit than the developing social science of anthropology, perhaps because it is more implicit in the first place, demanding an activity of interpretation rather than offering anything much in the way of propositional statements. The preceding historical and theoretical connections between fetishism (or totemism) and phallicism do, however, seem helpful in identifying the context of, for example, Dickens's analysis of the alienating functions of representation in a fetishized society. This alienation is evident even when the choice of an image is apparently self-elected; self and society are mutually determining. Mr. Turveydrop's figurative residence atop the "imaginary pinnacle" instances an alienation that is all the more horrifying because it is not brought to consciousness by any of those who suffer from it. There is no potential for correction, as there might be with Dombey's "little image," who is capable of inward deviation even as he outwardly reflects the father's posture. Paul Dombey's questions about money fracture the narcissistic aspiration projected by his father. Dombey also seeks to extinguish the presence and identity of the female, another force that threatens the integrity of the image, and he enlists the services of Mr. Carker in this respect. Here too the 'other' emerges in revolt, though it is revolt by reduplication. Having been for so long a dinner-table witness to Dombey's hegemony enacted in the public humiliation of his wife, Carker is denied self-dependence by the 'Murdstone' principle of exclusive firmness. But the tributary firmness eventually fights back, and Edith of course becomes imaginatively enmeshed in his revenge against the master. Truly corrupted, Carker too can only assert himself by displaying his own capacity to humiliate others.

He thereby demonstrates a process already described by Godwin:

> But to be the subject of an individual, of a being with the same form, and the same imperfections as myself; how much must the human mind be degraded, how much must his grandeur and independence be emasculated, before I can learn to think of this with patience, with indifference, nay, as some men do, with pride and exultation? Such is the idol that monarchy worships, in lieu of the divinity of truth, and the sacred obligation of public good. . . . May we bend the knee before the shrine of vanity and folly without injury? Far otherwise. Mind had its beginning

in sensation, and it depends upon words and symbols for the progress of its associations. The truly good man must not only have a heart resolved, but a front erect. We cannot practise abjection, hypocrisy and meanness, without becoming degraded in other men's eyes and in our own.

(*Enquiry*)

The emasculation, the unmanning of the "front erect," takes place by the transference of the image of firmness to another human being, the king. As that which now excites worship, the king becomes the essential self of the worshipper. The truly independent man must have not just the inward identity of self-subsistence, the "heart resolved," but also the outward image, the "front erect." Because the mind grows by words and symbols, he must maintain the *image* within his control, lest he subsequently lose the inward condition that that image speaks forth. It is not possible, within this idea of the mind, to retain the one without the other. The standard quietism, which recommends the ignoring of outward, worldly relations and signs for the sake of authenticity within, is here discounted. We cannot ignore the demands of kings and priests, nor displace them as having merely superficial implications. There is a direct reciprocity between surface and content, as there was, implicitly, for Wordsworth in his retrospective analysis of the effects of carrying the surplice, the badge of belonging. Godwin's language here suggests that sexual dominance and passivity are implicated in the master-slave relationship and the forms of imaginary relation which it generates.

I now pass on to *Moby-Dick*. To say that the novel is about the male imagination is to say nothing new; and, insofar as it is also about phallicism, one can only marvel at the directness of the indirection. The quest of the *Pequod* is a quest for completion, for the capture of what is lacking, and it incorporates within the sphere of its ambitions everything from abstract knowledge of the most apparently dispassionate sort to commercial prosperity and the urge for gain. The various levels of the quest interact and even conflict with each other, and there is no sure way of keeping them apart, either in fact or in theory. We must never forget, also—as I shall often perhaps seem to forget for the purposes of this exposition—that Ahab, however demonic and outrageous his behavior might seem, has already, as a matter of fact, before the story begins, been robbed of his leg, and probably of something else besides, by the white whale. If the figuring mind takes twists and turns beyond what we might think of as the normal, then we should not forget the rationale that Melville has written into the factual elements of Ahab's past. What may be more open to question, I think, is the nature of the appeal Ahab extends to the crew, and to Ishmael. For this is a world of idols, in which all characters move and have their being. Queequeg's idol is an obvious idol, but whales are idols too, analogues of human self-completion. Thus Ishmael meditates at the masthead:

> There you stand, a hundred feet above the silent decks, striding along the deep, as if the masts were gigantic stilts, while beneath you and between your legs, as it were, swim the hugest monsters of the sea, even as ships once sailed between the boots of the famous Colossus at old Rhodes.
>
> (ch. 35)

He inscribes himself into a position of absolute power, with all created things "beneath" as attributes of his identity; but the image is perfectly balanced, for it implies both control over what is swimming between the legs (possession), and also terror, fear of losing what is already possessed to other, free floating, forms. Melville here conveys the dialectic of mastery and slavery at a single stroke, and it is resolved for Ishmael by inactivity and repetition. The phantasized omnipotence of life at the masthead is offset by the physical discomfort of being there—"so sadly destitute of anything approaching a cosy inhabitiveness"—as well as by the inverse intuition of having *nothing* under the feet, between the legs. The superimposition of everything and nothing produces a "languor" and a suspension of discriminating consciousness which leads to the calenture, a description of which, along with the death wish implicit in it, ends this chapter, as a warning to the aspiring Pantheist not to depart from the sense of distinct identity. This separate self may indeed impose an anguish of individuality (which Ishmael seeks to overcome in bonding with the society of the ship) and its public dimension, a personalized misreading of the world; but, it is suggested, it is all we have if we are to remain alive. Consciousness is a fact, to be cancelled only by the fact of death.

Of all the forms that float between Ishmael's legs, the white whale is the most overburdened with human aspirations and self-images. Indeed, it is crucial that Moby-Dick, who has already been set apart by being named— "Sir sailor, but do whales have christenings?" (ch. 54)—is *not* completely white. The white patch upon his brow is made to represent and mythologize him as white; the part is made to stand for the whole. He too is worked upon by this compulsive habit of alienated humanity, by being imaged into a form that distinguishes him most efficiently from other whales, and heightens his emblematic potential as a receiver of human readings. The actual, observed features of the whale are only partially, emblematically, white. He has "a peculiar snow-white wrinkled forehead, and a high, pyramidical white hump." These are his "prominent features," the "tokens whereby . . . he revealed his identity." The rest of his body is indeed "streaked, and spotted, and marbled with the same shrouded hue" (ch. 41), but it is the parts that Melville chooses to stress, in a way that distances his account from that in the sources he apparently drew upon, wherein the whale is described as "of the purest, most brilliant white," or, in another instance, *"white as wool!"* It is the taking of part for whole that we are to register, entangled as it is in the mesh of rumors and metaphysical speculations that make up the chapter devoted to Moby-Dick (ch. 41).

As Moby-Dick in particular, so whales in general are objects for figuring. The very name of the species, the "sperm whale," is "philologically considered . . . absurd." The name had its origin in the idea that "this same spermaceti was that quickening humor of the Greenland Whale which the first syllable of the word literally expresses." When this myth was exposed, the "original name was still retained by the dealers; no doubt to enhance its value by a notion so strangely significant of its scarcity" (ch. 32). The poor beast is, it seems, doomed from the start as the focus of the most grandiose phantasies of potency, cunningly maintained as they are by those earning a living from its exploitation. Attempting to replace this mythology by something more scientific, Ishmael is obliged to give up the task of taxonimized parts, "detached bodily distinctions," in favor of a simple division by size. The true whale is unavailable, except in "volume" and thus exists as the sounding board for the genesis of an imaginary science, one that casts its findings in the most desired terms of companionship. It is the head of the whale which contains the precious oil, casing it within an "enormous boneless mass" of a toughness "inestimable by any man who has not handled it." This head has an "unobstructed elasticity" because it is "susceptible to atmospheric distension and contraction," and it is directed by the "mass of tremendous life" behind it. Thus the whale's "concentrations of potency," and the "irresistibleness of that might" (ch. 76), are teasingly imaged forth as parts having not a bone in them.

The whale is an "expansive monster" indeed. In the discussion of "The Nut" (ch. 80), Ishmael tries to answer his own question;

> How may unlettered Ishmael hope to read the awful Chaldee of the Sperm Whale's brow? I but put that brow before you. Read it if you can.
>
> (ch. 79)

Put it before us he does; "phrenologically" speaking, the head is "an entire delusion," and the whale "wears a false brow to the common world" (ch. 80). For the brain is very small, hidden away inside the skull, not represented on the surface. Ishmael, correspondingly, seeks to emphasize "the wonderful comparative magnitude of his spinal cord" as a measure of identity. For this *is* represented, by the hump, the proper emblem of the firm column that makes up the whale's personality: "From its relative situation then, I should call this high hump the organ of firmness or indomitableness in the Sperm Whale." This reading of the whale is of course a representation, and one that seems to function at the service of specific interests. The murdering by dissection reconstructs the whale as an efficient image of the phallus. The hump is always firm and always *seen* to be firm; the other "organ of firmness" is neither. Thus the ship's carpenter, "manmaker," refashioning Ahab's stiff leg, adverts to the refiguring of the human form which both sets in motion the quest and is further modified by it: "That is hard which should be soft, and that is soft which should be hard" (ch. 108). And Ahab, bitterly exercised by the mixture of recollected sensation and actual absence, threatens to order "a complete man after a desirable pattern."

Moby-Dick, however, who is more beautiful than "the white bull Jupiter" (ch. 133), does not subscribe to defeat, and he therefore remains to illuminate the pattern of desire that fuels the quest. That desire is necessarily only a desire for the *image*, at least as far as Ahab is concerned, and this in turn is only represented by substitution, as we have seen. For most of the time Moby-Dick withholds "from sight the full terrors of his submerged trunk," refusing to accede to the demand for full exposure, 'utterance,' and the control of the image (if *only* the image) which might be satisfied by revelation. He taunts Ahab, indeed, with this refusal to reveal, and does so again in the "pitchpoling" phenomenon that occurs when Moby-Dick has Ahab absolutely at his mercy:

> vertically thrusting his oblong white head up and down in the billows; and at the same time slowly revolving his whole spindled body; so that when his vast wrinkled forehead rose— some twenty or more feet out of the water—the now rising swells, with all their confluent waves, dazzlingly broke against it.
>
> (ch. 133)

This is also a grotesque and acquiescent parody of what Ahab cannot do; for Moby-Dick, as well as condemning Ahab to that unnaturally hard ivory leg, has probably robbed him of another unmentioned member:

all loveliness is anguish to me, since I can ne'er enjoy. Gifted
with the high perception, I lack the low, enjoying power;
damned, most subtly and most malignantly! damned in the midst
of Paradise!

(ch. 37)

Harold Beaver has pointed out that Queequeg's overtly phallic idol, Yojo,
is named as a palindrome of "O joy." Ahab's inability to experience joy,
which is what the whale perpetuates in refusing (or so it seems) to kill him
off when it first has the chance, condemns him to an unending quest for
substitutes. The ship's carpenter speaks again:

"Seems to me some sort of Equator cuts yon old man, too, right
in his middle. He's always under the Line—fiery hot, I tell ye!"

(ch. 127)

The devil's all below; but only by substitution, by proxy, through a companionable form. The paradoxical identity of Moby-Dick consists in the
doubling of motives whereby he is both the object on whom revenge must
be taken and at the same time the image of the lost member which must
be conquered and regained. Outer form and inner impulse, cause and effect,
are in conjunction here, and . . . we cannot be sure that Melville means to
encourage any simple criticism or moral animus against the incomplete
Ahab. Whatever compulsions he obeys in figuring the whale, there seems
little doubt that it has given him ample motive.

In a peculiar way, Ahab and Moby-Dick are doubles; at least they are
so figured by Ishmael. At first sight, Ishmael is appalled by Ahab, just as
he will be by the whale. Ahab has a mark on his face which is "lividly
whitish," and we are soon told "that for the first few moments I hardly
noted that not a little of this overbearing grimness was owing to the barbaric
white leg upon which he partly stood" (ch. 28). As we shall see, Moby-
Dick's whiteness occasions a long disquisition on the horror caused by that
color, or absence of color. Ahab comes to identify with the whale, "not
only all his bodily woes, but all his intellectual and spiritual exasperations"
(ch. 41). The reflexivity implicit in his threat, "I will dismember my dis-
memberer" (ch. 37), is enacted also in the mirror imaging of the body-
parts that they project to the outer world. As Moby-Dick shows a "wrinkled
brow" (ch. 36, ch. 44) or "wrinkled forehead" (ch. 41) as the sign of his
identity, so Ahab too shows a "wrinkled brow, till it almost seemed that
while he himself was marking out lines and courses on the wrinkled charts,
some invisible pencil was also tracing lines and courses upon the deeply
marked chart of his forehead" (ch. 44). As his "snow-white new ivory leg"

matches the whale's hump, so, when he goes back to the charts, it is again with a "wrinkling" of the brow (ch. 109), reading himself thus into an imitative (and thus worshipful) relation to the figure of his pursuit. It is Ahab's "unappeasable brow" (ch. 135) that Starbuck sees with his last earthly glance, as he too is mesmerized into the circle of duplication and compulsion, to his death. Thus operates the mirrorlike dialectic of fetishism.

However negatively or positively we read Ahab's relation to the white whale, it is clearly a relation dependent upon substitution and reflection rather than upon achievement and conjunction. This pertains even in death. It is the Parsee, himself always written into an almost magnetic connection with his captain, who dies the death most properly befitting Ahab himself, strapped by the harpoon line to the whale's back, his "half torn body" (ch. 135) thus disjunctively connected to the object that his master has in such a tortured way worshipped and hated for so long. Man and whale belong together, but only in a metonymic relationship, held by rope. That is the answer to the assumption of control Ahab seeks in his revenge—so suffer all men wedded to their tools—and it is itself presented *to* him rather than enacted *by* him. Ahab is thus made to see, at a distance, his own predicament of distance *imaged* in the Parsee. For Ahab himself dies in utter silence, strangled and dragged from the boat, though not before he has commented on the final disjunction or distance forced upon him, dying away from his ship, "cut off from the last fond pride of meanest shipwrecked captains." Always cut off.

This is indeed a book about substitution on the grandest scale, and not just in the personalized context of Ahab's quest. Just as the collected etymologies and the various data which preface the story do not encapsulate the whale, so none among the activities of deflection and representation taking place in the narrative ever manages to produce that apparently sought-for "full utterance"—the phrase is Conrad's, as we shall see [elsewhere]. Ahab tries to integrate Moby-Dick into the most familiar and apparently manageable form of social exchange and shared meanings, the money system, in offering the doubloon as the reward for the first sighting. But this gesture is at once undermined by the 'mad' discourse of the ship's boy, Pip, as he sees it nailed to the mast:

> "Here's the ship's navel, this doubloon here, and they are all on fire to unscrew it. But, unscrew your navel, and what's the consequence? Then again, if it stays here, that is ugly, too, for when aught's nailed to the mast it's a sign that things grow desperate. Ha, ha! old Ahab! the White Whale; he'll nail ye!"
>
> (ch. 99)

Reference to the old joke, of which most editors remind us (but which in fact invites reference to the falling off of more than one body-part), highlights the prospect of loss within the sign which asks to be taken as gain. The sighting of the whale thus threatens the dismembering of the ship and of all who sail in her. But the ship is already committed to disaster, by the fact of the nailing to the mast, the concentration of energy into a single, obsessive direction. And the doubloon is in fact not at all a principle of exchange but yet another example of Ahab redoubling himself. No other sailor manages to anticipate him in spotting the white whale, so that the reward he has offered in fact devolves on himself: "No, the doubloon is mine, Fate reserved the doubloon for me. *I* only; none of ye could have raised the White Whale first" (ch. 133). The coin is his image, the thing that purports to be outside him, but that is in fact within in its essential purposes. Thus, when he fixed his "riveted glance" on the "riveted gold coin," he too "wore the same aspect of nailed firmness" (ch. 99). Within is without, for Ahab.

That the crew accept and respond to this challenge may speak for their complicity, reluctant or otherwise, in Ahab's quest. There is a way, indeed, in which their very presence on the ship suggests an acceptance of the cycle of substitution on which that quest is based. Ishmael and Queequeg began by being wedded, figuratively, as a "cosy, loving pair" (ch. 10), and that wedding is a microcosm of the society of the ship as a whole. Whatever level of self-election might have been involved at the start of the voyage, there is no doubt that Ahab's despotic captaincy makes it hard for the crew to resist him; at the same time, this is not of itself enough to account for the continuance of the quest. For in revealing the purpose of the voyage to be the single-minded pursuit of the one white whale, Ahab has "directly laid himself open to the unanswerable charge of usurpation," to the point where the crew could "refuse all further obedience to him, and even violently wrest from him the command" (ch. 46). Ahab must thus instil into them the same sense of purpose he feels in himself: "your own condescension, *that* shall bend ye to it. I do not order ye; ye will it" (ch. 36). Melville may here be suggesting something akin to Godwin's insight into the inwardly eroding function of the outward image of authority. The man who lives under a king cannot be capable of independent decision and cannot but be bent to the purposes of those who rule over him. To resist authority would be to fight against that tendency in himself which approves and identifies with the images of power. Additionally, it may be that the images Ahab does invoke appeal to a common conviction in the crew—all men, after all—so that they identify with the fitness of the quest. Whatever the reason, when the chase is on, the crew of the *Pequod* become as the obedient limbs of Ahab's body, organic substitutes for what he does not have;

> They were one man, not thirty. For as the one ship that held them all; though it was put together of all contrasting things— oak, and maple, and pine wood; iron, and pitch, and hemp— yet all these ran into each other in the one concrete hull, which shot on its way, both balanced and directed by the long central keel; even so, all the individualities of the crew, this man's valor, that man's fear; guilt and guiltiness, all varities were welded into oneness, and were all directed to that fatal goal which Ahab their one lord and keel did point to.
>
> (ch. 134)

Here the many are reduced to the one, variety to conformity, the polymorphous to the fixated, to the "long central keel" that is the vehicle of Ahab's monomania. Ahab becomes the vehicle of the others' energies, their "keel." The act of irresistible will directs all ulterior motives to itself, and destroys the differences that would offer a basis for doubt or debate. In the case of most of the members of the crew, Melville gives us nothing to allow us to distinguish choice from necessity in their having become whalers; but at this moment, all such questions are redundant.

Even at less active moments, the task of sorting out the outwardly determined from the inwardly (socially or individually) projected seems an impossible one. We have no sure methods for telling apart what is enforced on people by environmental and technological necessity and what is the product of the compulsive urge for companionable form. For example, the investment in images is quite literal for the "mincer," who tailorizes himself into, "slips himself bodily into," the inverted skin of the whale's penis, "that unaccountable cone," the "grandissimus" which was in olden times an idol; at least its "likeness" was (ch. 95). The practical and the imaginative are coinstantaneous, impossible to sort into cause and effect. This "cassock" may indeed be the one thing that will "adequately protect" the mincer in his particular job, but it is also a magical-religious "investiture" that is "Immemorial to all his order;" it is an assumption of "canonicals." Technology usurps natural sexual functions in order to exploit nature the more efficiently; it does so by figuratively casting itself as embodied sexuality.

In this way the commercial questing of the whale is enwrapped within a deeper aspiration whose exact limits are never spoken to us. Jest and earnest, cruelty and suffering, man dwarfed by nature or man digesting it to his purposes, these options and extremes are not presented to us in terms

of a propositional moral decision. Appropriately, all of Ishmael's meditations on and around whales proceed by analogy rather than by assertive
evidence. The object of definition can never be presented or essentialized;
it exists rather as a series of infinitely deflected schemas and possibilities.
Chapters 55 through 57 are mostly about what the whale is not, a history
of the various misrepresentations that have gathered around it. The educated
whaleman sees whales everywhere; in the stars, in the mountains, and so
forth. But these are only "images," whether of a monomaniac preoccu-
pation or a habitual association. Too much whaling makes one see only
whales. It is the revenge of divided labor that an alternative reality is ungraspable, or ceases to exist. But it is also in the nature of whales proper
that they refuse to be decisively imaged, so that

> you must needs conclude that the great Leviathan is that one
> creature in the world which must remain unpainted to the last.
> True, one portrait may hit the mark much nearer than another,
> but none can hit it with any considerable degree of exactness.
> So there is no earthly way of finding out precisely what the
> whale really looks like. And the only mode in which you can
> derive even a tolerable idea of his living contour, is by going a
> whaling yourself; but by so doing, you run no small risk of
> being eternally stove and sunk by him. Wherefore, it seems to
> me you had best not to be too fastidious in your curiosity touch-
> ing this Leviathan.
>
> (ch. 55)

Even visual contact does not produce such sought-for knowledge, merely
a "tolerable idea" of the "contour."

Ishmael's appetite for the companionship of outward images is as compulsive as anyone else's, though a good deal less aggressive than Ahab's.
In the midst of the most apparently dispassionate of all appreciations of
natural beauty and the self-subsistence of other living things, that of the
"young Leviathan amours in the deep," he is yet able to exercise the process
of self-imaging in the subaqueous paradise beneath him:

> But even so, amid the tornadoed Atlantic of my being, do I
> myself still for ever centrally disport in mute calm; and while
> ponderous planets of unwaning woe revolve around me, deep
> down and deep inland there I still bathe me in eternal mildness
> of joy.
>
> (ch. 87)

Joy again, and as so often in this book, it is of the implicitly sexual sort. Ishmael is, however, a more open spirit than I might seem to be suggesting here. He sees the agony of the dying whale, even as he sees also "enough to appal the stoutest man who so pitied" (ch. 81), and above all perhaps he asserts the criminality of the aspiration towards completion and full utterance, its blasphemous impossibility: "I promise nothing complete; because any human thing supposed to be complete, must for that very reason infallibly be faulty" (ch. 32).

The locus of this quest for completion in the logic of phallicism, seen already in Ahab, is intuited more academically by Ishmael too, his

> cetological System standing thus unfinished, even as the great Cathedral of Cologne was left, with the crane still standing upon the top of the uncompleted tower. For small erections may be finished by their first architects; grand ones, true ones, ever leave the copestone to posterity. God keep me from ever completing anything. This whole book is but a draught—nay, but the draught of a draught. Oh, Time, Strength, Cash, and Patience!
>
> (ch. 32)

Melville seems to have chosen the richer of the two spellings open to him. The word *draught* occupies seven columns in the *OED*, and most of its meanings can be played into this passage and the book from which it comes. The process of definition is itself a vortex drawing us away from the aspiration to "finish" which the passage as a whole comments upon. The writer's art, positioned between first drafts and bank drafts (to use the more usual modern spelling), is itself defined within the metaphysical predicament of unfinishing, relief from which may be found in the draught of poison or the draught of wine. And is it all an exhalation of air, consigned to a privy? Thus all master builders?

The unfinishing goes on, and the mandatory incompletion of great erections touches on the traditional connection of sexual self-consciousness with the myth of the fall of man. Incompletion and endless aspiration are the fate of man outside Eden (women less so!), just as the sexual identity is thrust upon his conscience by the knowledge of transgression. At the level of the whaling industry as a whole (itself an image of territorial expansion and man's attempt to discipline nature, to cultivate or exploit the unparadisal earth), incompletion is reflected again in Ishmael's faith that the whale will *survive*. Ironic as it may seem to us today, he contrasts the whale with the buffalo, already as good as extinct with the progress of America's push westwards, and concludes that it will fare otherwise, and that it possesses the means to "bid defiance to all pursuit from man" (ch. 105). Not only will it elude definition, Ishmael seems to suggest, but also man's pursuit to destroy it and to convert it completely to his purposes. This enables the whale, and Moby-Dick in particular, to function in the book as a rebuttal of both man's commercial greed and his possessive imagination. There will be something left when the whalers of this world have finished—something analogous, perhaps, to those "charms" and "mysteries" of which Melville spoke in the passage that stands as the epigraph to this chapter. Moby-Dick always has a life of his own. At one time he seems malevolent and purposeful, in ways that the human imagination can identify, at another he behaves in a way that speaks for utter indifference and self-containment, outside the scope of mankind's intentional projections. He is the fetish who is, like all fetishes, both admired and hated (or feared), but he also earns from Ishmael an independence from such a dialectic. Insofar as he is *not* destroyed, then the human quest itself comes to be, perversely, tinged with the heroism of a challenge to the unknowable and the impossible. Ishmael, in consequence, need never be quite the completely innocent observer touched on by Nietzsche at the opening of *The Will to Power*:

> He that speaks here, conversely, has done nothing so far but reflect: a philosopher and solitary by instinct, who has found his advantage in standing aside and outside, in patience, in procrastination, in staying behind . . . the first perfect nihilist of Europe who, however, has even now lived through the whole of nihilism, to the end, leaving it behind, outside himself.

He is indeed rewarded for his comparative effacement from the scene of critical action and critical transgression by being allowed to fall behind, to survive both whales and sharks, and to tell his tale. He is the orphan picked up by the *Rachel* at the end of the book. And, if his name alludes to the wild outcast of Genesis (16:12) invoked already in Fenimore Cooper's *The Prairie*, must this not be an ironic identification as applied to this whimsical sailor, who survives buoyed up on a floating coffin to tell his tale?

But despite these intimations of the incorporeal, Ishmael is not Nietzsche's "perfect nihilist." He too is a hunter of whales, and he is in admiration of Ahab's hatred of and search for that "inscrutable thing" (ch. 36) he sees in the white whale. For Ahab offers the demonic (and potentially creative) prospect of it *not* being necessary to accept our shortcomings. The obverse of the energy of destruction is always that of civilization:

> But, as in his narrow-flowing monomania, not one jot of Ahab's
> broad madness had been left behind; so in that broad madness,
> not one jot of his great natural intellect had perished. That before
> living agent, now became the living instrument.
>
> (ch. 41)

Agent to instrument, obscure, generative radical to utilitarian tool, idea to image, spirit to matter. Ahab's acts speak for the misapplication and reduction to fixity of what Coleridge called the "living Power and prime Agent of all human Perception" (*Biographia* 1. 202). Some degree of such fixity may, however, be necessary to all significant action. Ahab goes too far, so that he, "to that one end, did now possess a thousand fold more potency than ever he had sanely brought to bear upon any one reasonable object" (ch. 41).

It is at least open to question, however, whether Ishmael goes far enough; for at times it seems close to the heart of Melville's ethic that we cannot live without significant action and the risks of transgression it involves. This deploying of active consciousness always exists in a state of tension for the Romantic and post-Romantic mind, and the argument for its necessity, as we have seen, must always draw a line to prevent itself approving of the more dangerous aspects of the Protestant aspiration, ever trying to complete itself into a prelapsarian state, to regain what it has (theorized as) inexorably lost. Just as a measure of this desire seems to be essential to all alternative constructions of order—and all orderings are constructed—so an excess of it directed at any one principle or component of such order alienates its possessor both from himself and from his community. The theory of knowledge in which this situation is contained insists on the presence of delirium at both ends of its spectrum. At one, there looms the prospect of monomania and fixation; at the other, random sensibility whose items are unconnected by *any* principle of succession or coherence. The Romantic ethic, as it appears in Wordworth's idea of the imagination, and in Schiller's of the aesthetic, insists in return on the mobile occupation of the middle ground between.

If there is a place for asking the question about whether Ishmael goes far enough—and I would not myself weight the novel in this direction—then it is created, as I have said, in part and perhaps largely because Moby-Dick *survives* to be sought again; he is not destroyed by the various species of human figurings, whether commercial or metaphysical. Ahab does convert his own "living agent" into a mere instrument, but he is not ultimately able to incorporate Moby-Dick into that conspiracy of self-consolidation. If he were, then we would have a precise example of the reifying function of the labor process as it is specified by Marx:

> In the labour process, therefore, man's activity, *via* the instruments of labour, effects an alteration in the object of labour which was intended from the outset. The process is extinguished in the product. The product of the process is a use-value, a piece of natural material adapted to human needs by means of a change in its form. Labour has become bound up in its object: labour has been objectified, the object has been worked on. What on the side of the worker appeared in the form of unrest [*Unruhe*] now appears, on the side of the product in the form of being [*Sein*], as a fixed, immobile characteristic. The worker has spun, and the product is a spinning.
>
> (*Capital*)

Ahab, in these terms, is the unsuccessful "worker" who is not able to transform the natural material into the desired product. Moby-Dick does not undergo any alteration; if he has a "being," then it is a fluent, indeterminate one, ever challenging and open to challenge. Ahab's energies in fact rebound upon himself, and the way in which *his* labor becomes "bound up" is, as we have seen, somewhat literal; he is strangled by a line from the whale's body, in a commemoration of the alienated and detached nature of the "work" he has tried to do on this object. The whale's escape may be an image of the hope or faith or myth that man's energies as worker will not succeed in turning the world into a gallery of dead commodities.

The faith in this escape legitimizes, I think, the *horror vacui* that Ishmael seems to sense, at times, in the prospect of a life without Ahab and his kind. It renders less than catastrophic the "wild, mystical, sympathetical feeling" that allows him to affirm that "Ahab's quenchless feud seemed mine" (ch. 41). In chapter 42, "The Whiteness of the Whale," Ishmael proceeds by conflating the accumulated cultural mythology of whiteness—"the intensifying agent in things the most appalling to mankind"—with the particular experience of the whale in a way that does not speak for any calling into question of his own self-consciousness; though of course we can provide that question for ourselves, insofar as he is a dramatic narrator. He is content to appeal to what he would have us take as instinct for the fearful intuition of "the nameless things of which the mystic sign gives forth such hints," and to a consensus of common experience for his final question: "Wonder ye then at the fiery hunt?" We have already seen that the whiteness of the whale is in fact a figuring, a reading of the parts as the whole, and this suggests that it is a psychological compulsion we are witnessing in the interpretation of all things white:

> Or is it, that as in essence whiteness is not so much a color as the visible absence of color, and at the same time the concrete of all colors; is it for these reasons that there is such a dumb blankness, full of meaning, in a wide landscape of snows—a colorless, all-color of atheism from which we shrink?
>
> (ch. 42)

Atheism, not pantheism. In its tolerance of all superimposed inscriptions, all choices, as equally superficial, equally a *reflection* rather than a reading into or a glance within, the whiteness is a denial of the trick and turn of mind whereby the inquiring or idling spirit pretends that its impositions of differences and forms are authorized readings of the world outside. Hence atheism, the denial of a licence for seeing, and for sharing.

I cannot claim to be able to historicize firmly Ishmael's terror before the prospect (or figment) of pure whiteness, but there are interesting analogues in Wordsworth, and in Goethe's *Theory of Colours*. Goethe notes the disorganizing effects of whiteness; a bright object appears larger than a dark one of the same size, and while the dark one leaves the "organ in a state of repose," the bright one "excites it." For

> the eye cannot for a moment remain in a particular state determined by the object it looks upon. On the contrary, it is forced to a sort of opposition, which, in contrasting extreme with extreme, intermediate degree with intermediate degree, at the same time combines these opposite impressions, and thus ever tends to a whole, whether the impressions are successive, or simultaneous and confined to one image.

Given that we construct form itself out of "light, shade, and colour," we can see here the prospect of an epistemology based in the figured representations built out of the interchange between eye and object, much as we find it in Wordsworth. What is so violent about absolute whiteness is that, as an extreme state, it inspires an equally extreme reaction in the effort to compose a mediated wholeness; this is an instance of "the silent resistance which every vital principle is forced to exhibit when any definite or immutable state is presented to it." In this way, though to a lesser degree, every "decided colour does a certain violence to the eye, and forces the organ to opposition."

Similarly, whiteness for Wordsworth was a principle of disorganization. Absent in nature, in its pure form, except "in small objects," its introduction into the landscape by man "destroys the *gradations* of distance":

> Five or six white houses, scattered over a valley, by their obtrusiveness, dot the surface, and divide it into triangles, or other mathematical figures, haunting the eye, and disturbing that repose which might otherwise be perfect.
>
> (Prose Works)

It subverts, in other words, that normative perspective that is based on the reading of depth and relation into the items placed before the eye, and placed in such a way as to contribute to the integration of that eye into the landscape beheld. Whiteness is in this sense a denial of power in its refusal to provide access to the depth of things, and to a principle of organization. Wordsworth's account of his journey through the Alps is pertinent here:

> That day we first
> Beheld the summit of Mont Blanc, and griev'd
> To have a soulless image on the eye
> Which had usurp'd upon a living thought
> That never more could be:
>
> (The Prelude 6.452–56)

Here, the *mind*'s eye had prefigured the mountain into a symbolic presence, part in and for whole, an organizing figure of power. That was the "living thought," but experience, like Moby-Dick, fights back and insists on its difference; the actual optical sensation, being a poor substitute for what the mind has come to of itself, thus comes to be cast as a "soulless image." The 'real' is an *image* when set against the intending mind's fulsome anticipations. The imagination's aspiration to compose into unity is rebuked by contingency, as the landscape will not bear that kind of efficient selectiveness. Mont Blanc, in fact, proves itself unviable as a symbol, and also as a fetish, in that it will not allow the mind to elide its *difference* from matter; the act of giving meaning is thrown right back in the face of the donor. As we read on, it becomes clear that it is the reintroduction of the many for the one—the reversal of the process that the mind alone has tried to enact—which reconciles the poet's disappointment:

> the wondrous Vale
> Of Chamouny did, on the following dawn,
> With its dumb cataracts and streams of ice,

> A motionless array of mighty waves,
> Five rivers broad and vast, make rich amends,
> And reconcil'd us to realities.
>
> (6.456–61)

The five make rich amends for the soleness and soullessness of the one. Wordsworth rebounds from blankness, from whiteness, to correct himself and, with the aid of an alternative nature, recreate the charitable space for human presence. Gradation is restored, albeit with the intimation of triteness in its prospect of embodied harmonies:

> There small birds warble from the leafy trees,
> The Eagle soareth in the element;
> There doth the reaper bind the yellow sheaf,
> The Maiden spread the haycock in the sun,
> While Winter like a tamed Lion walks
> Descending from the mountain to make sport
> Among the cottages by beds of flowers.
>
> (6.462–68)

This somewhat humdrum listing of the items of the familiar landscape is a relief from the all-absorbing vacancy of whiteness, all-color and no color. Whiteness, like Hebrew theology, does not allow for representation. It is the image of infinity, and it is the death of the single self. If this is the coding of whiteness in *Moby-Dick*, then it makes the white whale both image and no-image. His shape and qualities attract the imagination, as his color thwarts and denies its operations; he is the fetish who compulsively attracts and inexorably disappoints, only to attract again. Whatever faltering there may be in Wordsworth's return to the lowlands, he does return. Ahab, and perhaps Ishmael too, remain with the soulless image, mesmerized, fixed, hateful, and worshipful. The "devious-cruising Rachel," searching for her own lost children, finds only another orphan in Ishmael (epilogue). Loss replicates loss, and finding emphasizes that loss. But at least Moby-Dick survives.

The Career of Ishmael's Self-Transcendence

Rowland A. Sherrill

In the opening chapter of *Moby-Dick*, Ishmael, whose very name refers to the "outcast," presents himself to the reader as a more desperate orphan than the young Wellingborough Redburn ever considered himself. For Redburn, hearth and home, mother and sisters, await him at the end of the journey, and the journey itself is undertaken at what is a more or less characteristic stage in an adolescent process of maturation. For Ishmael, the sea voyage is the only logical sequel except for suicide to a life which seems to be getting "gray and grizzled":

> Whenever I find myself growing grim about the mouth; when-
> ever it is a damp, drizzly November in my soul; whenever I
> find myself involuntarily pausing before coffin warehouses, and
> bringing up the rear of every funeral I meet; and especially when-
> ever my hypos get such an upper hand of me, that it requires a
> strong moral principle to prevent me from deliberately stepping
> into the street, and methodically knocking people's hats off—
> then, I account it high time to get to sea as soon as I can. This
> is my substitute for pistol and ball. With a philosophical flourish
> Cato throws himself upon his sword; I quietly take to the ship.
>
> (ch. 1)

As Tommo came slowly to learn in *Typee*, then, the world of human life is radically fallen, and Ishmael inherits this fallen condition from his pre-

From *The Prophetic Melville: Experience, Transcendence and Tragedy,* © 1979 by the University of Georgia Press. Originally entitled "The Span of Portents: The Career of Ishmael's Self-Transcendence."

decessor not as a doctrine to which he gives intellectual assent but as a fact of experience itself, felt in the "drizzly November in my soul." Severed from the kind of experience which would support and enrich his life, he remembers, in his retrospection, having been pulled toward the sea, having himself been one of those "thousands upon thousands of mortal men fixed in ocean reveries," and having been brought by adversity and woe to "the extremest limit of the land" (ch. 1).

In its continuity with the lives portrayed in the early works, then, Ishmael's life, while it cannot refuse the "fall" finally recognized by Tommo, also inherits the possibility of reconciliation with experience hypothesized, if not fully possessed, by young Redburn. For Ishmael, "grim about the mouth" as he recalled himself to be, the sea withholds such a promise to redeem life for him; why go to sea to avoid "pistol and ball," he asks rhetorically:

> Why did the poor poet of Tennessee, upon suddenly receiving two handfuls of silver, deliberate whether to buy him a coat, which he sadly needed, or invest his money in a pedestrian trip to Rockaway Beach? Why is almost every robust healthy boy with a robust healthy soul in him, at some time or other crazy to go to sea? Why upon your first voyage as a passenger, did you yourself feel such a mystical vibration, when first told that you and your ship were now out of sight of land? Why did the old Persians hold the sea holy? Why did the Greeks give it a separate deity, and make him the own brother of Jove? Surely all this is not without meaning.
>
> (ch. 1)

Having suffered experience which has blighted and scarred him, Ishmael is allured, even driven, to "water gazing": "as every one knows," he says, "meditation and water are wedded for ever" (ch. 1). His voyage is for recuperation: he wants not to recover from some physical ailment but, rather, to recover himself in relation to the holy by meditating on oceanic revelations. However, despite the assertive tone of voice—"as every one knows"—Ishmael, as he presents himself in the early pages of his narrative, can only hope for such a recovery of spirit for his life, can only hope when the flood-gates are swung open to him that he will find in all that sea-room the exhilarated world of wonder which will answer to the need of his life. He searches for the portents of the transcendent which had earlier presented themselves to the experience of Tommo and Redburn, but he is a seeker and not a finder yet.

Now, Ishmael's fallen situation, his previous buffeting at the hands of experience, and, indeed, the fact of his seeking, figure cumulatively as the crucial condition which he hopes will be surmounted by his passage through "the great flood-gates of the wonder-world" (ch. 1). He wants to meditate on the world of experience in its strange, unloosed, and allusive quality—wants to seize "the image of the ungraspable phantom of life" (ch. 1)—and, in these meditations, to find that which will enable him to reconcile himself to life. By searching his experience at "the level of *theos*, or ultimate meaning," he hopes to transcend the condition of woe which hems him in, and his seeking, definitive as it is of his fallen life, is the first stage in the career of his self-transcendence. His hope for the wonder-world will, by the end of the narrative, become a faith in the truth of such a revelatory world, and Ishmael, in a slow and frequently halting way, will have learned how to respond commensurately to the promise and demand of such a world, will have learned how to experience it fully. In the portentous world, such a version of full experiencing—of self-transcendence—is achieved by taking "the span of portents" as Melville's persona expresses it in the poem "In a Bye-Canal" (1891):

> Fronted I have, part taken the span
> of portents in nature and peril in man.
> I have swum—I have been
> 'Twixt the whale's black flukes and the white shark's fin.

The "span" includes a process or pattern of expectation, discovery, scrutiny, and possession of the "portents in nature"—a process, for Ishmael, which issues in the location of a context of ultimacy wherein to find new meaning for his life. But a part of this pattern includes Ishmael's assessing the "peril" in himself and in other men which stands in its variety of forms, as an obstacle to full experiencing and self-transcendence.

If the retrospective narrator of *Moby-Dick* presents an unaccustomed world, his account also records the version of self-transcendence which is defined by the course of Ishmael's active progress in the narrative from hope in the reality of such a wonder-world to faith in the truth of such a world discovered as *kairos* and symbol. The narrative opens, however, with Ishmael's false starts into the watery groves of our Thessalies and the ways in which he overcomes these initial perils as he encounters a variety of those abundant moments, which become the objects of his "gazing," and the spirit portended by them, which is the goal of his questing. These early encounters stand as propaedeutics, for their deep resonances teach him what will be necessary for his stance in relation to the great whale whose "island bulk"—whose "portentous and mysterious" aspect—makes it a symbol of the created order itself. In his metaphysical searching of the whale, the active Ishmael discovers both the limits on his epistemology and the real presence of the hidden God. Finally, in the attempt to possess the significance of his experience—by means of the narrative itself—Ishmael learns that life has, within its own keeping, a redemptive element for the man who has eyes for it, and in this he learns also how to transcend "the fine hammered steel of woe" (ch. 96).

I

As Ishmael prepares to embark on his "voyage of recovery," he runs immediately against two "perils in man" which stand as obstacles to the full experience of the wondrous—the temptation to mediate experience through secondhand authorities and the narcissistic impulse to project himself on his experience. The etymological account of the word *whale* and the extracts on the subject of the whale both precede the narrative proper and present—in coming to terms with the portentous whale—a hurdle to the direct encounter which enables the most integral response to the whale itself. As means for deciphering the mysterious riddle of the whale, the etymology points out the relativity of language, and the extracts suggest the ambiguity in relative human perceptions. Both figure as confidence-dissolving elements which leave the figure of the great whale even more arcane than before. In the face of such an enigmatic figurement—which was, Ishmael recalls, chief among his motives for going to sea—Ishmael inclines for a time to the second peril. When all meaning appears to be relative, when the possibility of objective knowledge seems lost, it is not surprising that knowledge, for Ishmael, comes to be understood as self-projection onto what is essentially indeterminate ground. His gazing into the water reflects only his self-image: he can become Narcissus, "who because he could not grasp the tormenting, mild image he saw in the fountain, plunged into it and was drowned" (ch. 1). Ishmael himself finds in his water-gazing what seems to be "the ungraspable phantom of life," his own reflection, and thinks for a time that "this is the key to it all" (ch. 1). These perils, then, are also elements of the condition of the self, for each points toward an ambiguous reality, and the second, narcissism, represents a potentially self-destructive alternative in the face of such a reality. But Ishmael indicates in the first two chapters of *Moby-Dick* that he quickly surmounted each of these hurdles to his full experiencing.

Dealing with experience in a secondhand way is simply not an alternative for Ishmael. He tells the reader that he never goes to sea as a passenger who has the experience of the journey mediated by the crew of the ship but, rather, prefers to treat the voyage firsthand before the mast. With bluff tone, he jokes about his reasons for travelling as sailor and not as officer: "I always go to sea as a sailor, because of the wholesome exercise and pure air of the forecastle deck. For as in this world, head winds are far more prevalent than winds from astern (that is, if you never violate the Pythagorean maxim), so for the most part the Commodore on the quarter-deck gets his atmosphere at second hand from the sailors on the forecastle. He thinks he breathes it first; but not so. In much the same way do the commonalty lead their leaders in many other things, at the same time that the leaders little suspect it" (ch. 1). The maxim, of course, is to avoid eating beans which cause flatulence, but regardless of his reasons for wanting to be upwind, to meet the elements of the sea directly, he fulfills the necessity to "front" his life as the persona of "In a Bye-Canal" recalls having done. It was Henry Thoreau, of course, who fleshed out the notion of "fronting" a few years later in *Walden*. In a memorable passage about his motives, he wrote:

> I went to the woods because I wished to live deliberately, to front only the essential facts of life, and see if I could not learn what it had to teach, and not, when I came to die, discover that I had not lived. I did not wish to live what was not life, living is so dear; nor did I wish to practise resignation, unless it was quite necessary. I wanted to live deep and suck out all the marrow of life, to live so sturdily and Spartan-like as to put to rout all that was not life, to cut a broad swath and shave close, to drive life into a corner, and reduce it to its lowest terms, and, if it proved to be mean, why then to get the whole and genuine meanness of it, and publish its meanness to the world; or if it were sublime, to know it by experience, and be able to give a true account of it in my next excursion.

Ishmael is similarly, if more desperately, motivated. He has no choice in the matter; indeed the very disinheritance signalled by his name precludes his relying on anyone but himself to encounter and to possess the realm of his experience.

Ishmael as quickly eludes the second peril of narcissism. In his insistence on fronting his experience, the portentous whale becomes the paramount element to be encountered. His own self-image—reflected by the water, that which he thinks is the key to it all in the first chapter—presents him with the image of the "ungraspable phantom of life." By the third chapter, however, this ungraspable phantom is not his own image simply mirrored back to him; it is, rather, that which he discovers "in the unequal cross-lights" and within the "unaccountable masses of shades and shadows" of the painting in The Spouter-Inn:

> But what most puzzled and confounded you was a long, limber, portentous, black mass of something hovering in the centre of the picture over three blue, dim, perpendicular lines floating in a nameless yeast. A boggy, soggy, squitchy picture truly, enough to drive a nervous man distracted. Yet was there a sort of indefinite, half-attained, unimaginable sublimity about it that fairly froze you to it, till you involuntarily took an oath with yourself to find out what that marvellous painting meant. Ever and anon a bright, but alas, deceptive idea would dart you through.—It's a Hyperborean winter scene.—It's the breaking-up of the ice-bound stream of Time. But at last all these fancies yielded to that one portentous something in the picture's midst. *That* once found out, and all the rest were plain. But stop; does it not bear a faint resemblance to a gigantic fish? even the great leviathan himself?
>
> (ch. 3)

It is at this point that Ishmael takes the oath "to find out what that marvellous painting meant" and that he begins to recognize that it will be plain only when he has once found out about great leviathan himself. The painting and that "something hovering in the centre" of it do not return to Ishmael only his own reflection; he fails to find himself in the picture and his projections onto the picture, his fancies, finally must yield to the recognition of the unknown and portentous other, the sublimity of which "fairly froze you to it." The whale itself portends the ungraspable phantom of life and toward the whale Ishmael directs his metaphysical energies. His temporary narcissism, like his momentary reliance on secondhand accounts, has been overcome: he needs to front the whale and to do so in a way which is alert to the whale's distinctive otherness.

Now, Ishmael will encounter other perils in man as the course of his voyaging continues, but, for a time at least, he has achieved the openness to encounters with the portentous which will enable him to embark on the watery wonder-world. Embark Ishmael *must*, for he soon learns in confronting the symbolic figurement of Bulkington's refusal of the lee shore that "all deep, earnest thinking is but the intrepid effort of the soul to keep the open independence of her sea" and that "in landlessness alone resides the highest truth, shoreless, indefinite as God" (ch. 23). It is better, Ishmael learns, to front "that howling infinite, than be ingloriously dashed upon the lee" (ch. 23). This is also one of the lessons Father Mapple extrapolates from his sermon on Jonah: one can refuse the whale only at the risk of being "swallowed up" by it. The second lesson, of course, is the one Ishmael has taken to heart in his telling of his tale: "To preach the Truth to the face of Falsehood' " (ch. 9), a lesson commensurate with Melville's sense of the reformative document he wanted *Moby-Dick* to be. Embark Ishmael *can,* for he has been touched in his bosom by Queequeg in another of those strange, portentous moments:

> As I sat there in that now lonely room; the fire burning low, in that mild stage when, after its first intensity has warmed the air, it then only glows to be looked at; the evening shades and phantoms gathering round the casements, and peering in upon us silent, solitary twain; the storm booming without in solemn swells; I began to be sensible of strange feelings. I felt a melting in me. No more my splintered heart and maddened hand were turned against the wolfish world. This soothing savage had redeemed it. There he sat, his very indifference speaking a nature in which there lurked no civilized hypocrisies and bland deceits. Wild he was; a very sight of sights to see; yet I began to feel myself mysteriously drawn towards him. And those same things that would have repelled most others, they were the very magnets that thus drew me.
>
> (ch. 10)

Ishmael begins to learn the reasons of the heart in the embrace of this "savage," begins to develop the receptivity to wonder which reason cannot completely fathom, and begins to find a principle of redemption within the precincts of experience. He sets sail aboard the *Pequod* on Christmas day in his pursuit of a new life, and he hears in Bildad's song, as they approach the "wintry ocean," words of "hope and fruition": "Never did those sweet words sound more sweetly to me than then. They were full of hope and fruition. Spite of this frigid winter night in the boisterous Atlantic, spite of my wet feet and wetter jacket, there was yet, it then seemed to me, many a pleasant haven in store; and meads and glades so eternally vernal, that the grass shot up by the spring, untrodden, unwilted, remains at midsummer" (ch. 22). When he is "boldly launched upon the deep" and "lost in its unshored, harborless immensities," (ch. 32) Ishmael will realize that the wonder-world is not only a "pleasant haven" in "midsummer" but the world as *kairos* and symbol, and he will learn in the face of these oceanic revelations to prepare for the promise and demand of the whale.

Receptive to wonder, Ishmael finds that portents of the transcendent come frequently and vibrantly in the course of the ordinary duration of time and profoundly displace that time. As he stands his dutiful and mundane round on the masthead, as he details its construction, history, lack of convenience, and so on, he finds himself living through a plenary moment, fecund with a symbolism which alludes to another dimension and with which he is allowed a glimpse into the heart of being itself:

> Lulled into such an opium-like listlessness of vacant, unconscious reverie is this absent-minded youth by the blending cadence of waves with thoughts, that at last he loses his identity; takes the mystic ocean at his feet for the visible image of that deep, blue, bottomless soul, pervading mankind and nature; and every strange, half-seen, gliding, beautiful thing that eludes him; every dimly-discovered, uprising fin of some undiscernible form, seems to him the embodiment of those elusive thoughts that only people the soul by continually flitting through it. In this enchanted mood, thy spirit ebbs away to whence it came; becomes diffused through time and space; like Wickliff's sprinkled Pantheistic ashes, forming at last a part of every shore the round globe over.
>
> There is no life in thee, now, except that rocking life imparted by a gently rolling ship; by her, borrowed from the sea; by the sea, from the inscrutable tides of God. But while this sleep, this dream is on ye, move your foot or hand an inch; slip your hold at all; and your identity comes back in horror. Over Descartian vortices you hover. And perhaps, at mid-day, in the fairest weather, with one half-throttled shriek you drop through that transparent air into the summer sea, no more to rise for ever. Heed it well, ye Pantheists!
>
> (ch. 35)

In this instance, erupting out of the stuff of chronological time, the signals of the presence of the transcendent appear in a form which commingles rapture and horror, which at once promise a blending with being, threaten to annihilate human being, and return "your identity . . . back in horror."

Later in the narrative, the habitual passage of time is again displaced by a period which is abundant with spirit and which, again, fills the heart with dread: after "days, weeks passed, and under easy sail, the ivory Pequod had slowly swept across four several cruising-grounds," the ship enters an area of wonder, there allured by "The Spirit-Spout": "It was while gliding through these latter waters that one serene and moonlight night, when all the waves rolled by like scrolls of silver; and, by their soft, suffusing seethings, made what seemed a silvery silence, not a solitude: on such a silent night a silvery jet was seen far in advance of the white bubbles at the bow. Lit up by the moon, it looked celestial; seemed some plumed and glittering god uprising from the sea" (ch. 51). But the "flitting apparition" disappears as quickly as it had come—"the silvery jet was no more seen that night" and "every sailor swore he saw it once, but not a second time" (ch. 51)—and ordinary time resumes, only again to be displaced:

> This midnight-spout had almost grown a forgotten thing, when, some days after, lo! at the same silent hour, it was again announced: again it was descried by all; but upon making sail to overtake it, once more it disappeared as if it had never been. And so it served us night after night, till no one heeded it but to wonder at it. Mysteriously jetted into the clear moonlight, or starlight, as the case might be; disappearing again for one whole day, or two days, or three; and somehow seeming at every distinct repetition to be advancing still further and further in our van, this solitary jet seemed for ever alluring us on.
>
> (ch. 51)

The alluring aspect, however, also evokes "a sense of peculiar dread . . . as if it were treacherously beckoning us on and on" in order to "rend us at last in the remotest and most savage seas" (ch. 51). Indeed, "the Cape winds began howling around us, and we rose and fell upon the long, troubled seas . . . [and] sharply bowed to the blast, and gored the dark waves." The spirit-spout presides over the period—"calm, snow-white, and unvarying; still directing its fountain of feathers to the sky; still beckoning us on from before, the solitary jet would at times be descried" (ch. 51). Here, then, Ishmael is presented with a time with its own special and self-contained periodicity, pregnant with its own resonance and implications. It is a time which supersedes his ability to devise it or even to evoke it; he can neither create nor fully contain it. It is both disclosive and furtive, and he can only receive it and attempt to place himself in relation to it.

Such portentous moments do not always present themselves in dread guise to Ishmael's experience, however, for they come intermittently in forms which give rise to ecstasy and peace. Spotting and pursuing a nation of whales herding together, Ishmael finds his low boat pulled into the innermost of the concentric circles they have formed, wherein are kept the cows and calves of the herd:

> These smaller whales—now and then visiting our becalmed boat from the margin of the lake—evinced a wondrous fearlessness and confidence, or else a still, becharmed panic which it was impossible not to marvel at. Like household dogs they came snuffling round us, right up to our gunwales, and touching them; till it almost seemed that some spell had suddenly domesticated them. Queequeg patted their foreheads; Starbuck scratched their backs with his lance; but fearful of the consequences, for the time refrained from darting it.
>
> But far beneath this wondrous world upon the surface, another and still stranger world met our eyes as we gazed over the side. For, suspended in those watery vaults, floated the forms of the nursing mothers of the whales, and those that by their enormous girth seemed shortly to become mothers. The lake, as I have hinted, was to a considerable depth exceedingly transparent; and as human infants while suckling will calmly and fixedly gaze away from the breast, as if leading two different lives at the time; and while yet drawing mortal nourishment, be still spiritually feasting upon some unearthly reminiscence;—even so did the young of these whales seem looking up towards us, but not at us, as if we were but a bit of Gulf-weed in their new-born sight.
>
> (ch. 87)

The moment, like the water of this central lake, is "exceedingly transparent," for in it the finite augurs a glimpse of the infinite: "another and still stranger world" is in part disclosed in the figurement of the newborn, "still spiritually feasting upon some unearthly reminiscence," not yet completely severed from that world into which they gaze. Ishmael realizes that, paradoxically, the world of frights and fears also contains peace and bliss, "as if from some mountain torrent we had slid into a serene valley lake" (ch. 87).

Further, in this moment, he says, "some of the subtlest secrets of the seas seemed divulged to us in this enchanted pond. We saw young Leviathan amours in the deep." This instance, instinct with significance like the moment on the masthead, also gives him something of himself: "And thus, though surrounded by circle upon circle of consternations and affrights, did these inscrutable creatures at the centre freely and fearlessly indulge in all peaceful concernments; yea, serenely revelled in dalliance and delight. But even so, amid the tornadoed Atlantic of my being, do I myself still for ever centrally disport in mute calm; and while ponderous planets of un-waning woe revolve round me, deep down and deep inland there I still bathe me in eternal mildness of joy" (ch. 87). Such moments, and the allusiveness they bear, are induplicable and impermanent, Ishmael has discovered; they contain and portend an uncanny element, and yet, as they converge on the life of man, they throw light all around, creating their own magnetism and demanding a wonderment appropriate for the transcendent dimension which imbues them. Such a distinctively religious view of time is also dramatized in Henry Thoreau's poem "Within the Circuit of This Plodding Life" (1842) as the persona articulates his sense of some "moments of an azure hue" which, for a time, displace plodding, mundane, ordinary time and stand as their "own memorial." He recalls, among others, "How in the shimmering noon of summer past/Some unrecorded beam slanted across/The upland pastures where the Johnswort grew," and he realizes that, "by God's cheap economy made rich," the world discloses itself in such moments of abundance. As Giles Gunn has written in another context, moments such as these make it possible "to recover a sense of that radiance which temporarily redeems life even as the flow of life itself bears it away."

Now, these luminous moments occur over and over again in *Moby-Dick*, and they both enable Ishmael to work through to a faith in the reality of the wonder-world and prepare him, though not in any consecutive way, to approach the great whale which is the paradigmatic symbol of such a world. From the frequent portents, he has learned by the time of his retrospective account that he can depend on the creation to appear to him in portentous form, as *kairos* and symbol, but he has learned as well that such a world is radically contingent because, although anything may become a vessel of the transcendent, the vessels themselves are not holy. He has discovered that, while the portents fade, their momentary presence has a commanding aspect which he cannot refuse. He has found that the forms of such presence can evoke in him feelings which range from dread and horror to rapture and peace, that such presence is wholly other than the human and does not necessarily come in images which satisfy the human senses of mercy and compassion. The fact that the portents in *Moby-Dick* occasion, at times, feelings of fear and dread only makes Ishmael's responses concordant with the aspect of the *tremendum* present in these instances. As Rudolf Otto writes, the manifestations of the holy never completely lose the element of "awe-fulness" and sublimity and the human encounter with this attribute can result in a deep shudder, as the soul, "held speechless, trembles inwardly to the farthest fibre of its being." Nonetheless, Ishmael has recognized that despite their profound otherness, which might at times call his being into question or might threaten to annihilate him, these revelatory moments can give him back his essential being by enabling him to situate himself more fully in relation with the mysterious contours of this transcendent dimension. In order for this relation to occur, he must, in short, respect the integrity of the other, must maintain his essential self, and must bring the two into full encounter by the interpretation of symbols. This is the function of symbolism, as Paul Ricoeur describes it, when the "symbol gives reason to think that the *Cogito* is within being, and not vice versa." He writes: "Every symbol is finally a hierophany, a manifestation of the bond between man and the sacred. Now in treating the symbol as a simple revealer of self-awareness, we cut it off from its ontological function; we pretend to believe that 'know thyself' is purely reflexive, whereas it is first of all an appeal by which each man is invited to situate himself better in being—in Greek terms, to 'be wise.' " And thus, Ricoeur suggests, "the symbol gives rise to thought"; thought, or interpretation, allows one to situate himself deeper in being, and this wisdom calls for a "second naiveté" in the sense that the thinking self discovers that its thinking does not make it "cease to share in the being that challenges it in every symbol." Melville recognized this function of the symbol and its possibilities of a reconciliation with being, for certainly Ishmael will achieve such a "second naiveté" after thoughtful interpretation of the symbolic world which everywhere encompasses him. The lesson will be taught to Ishmael by the encompassing wonder-world through which he moves and will be confirmed when he engages and attempts to decipher the whale. Indeed, that portentous and mysterious monster will teach him further lessons still.

II

From first to last, Ishmael's narrative seeks to possess the significance of the whale, for, in order to decipher the "marvelous painting," the object toward which he "involuntarily took an oath," he must grasp "that one portentous something in the picture's midst," for "*that* once found out, and all the rest were plain" (ch. 1). He bends all his energies to the scrutiny of the whale and entertains all the varieties of inquiry which, cumulatively, he thinks will illumine the phantom of life by explicating that which resides at its center. The etymological tracings and the extracts which precede the narrative stand as the mode of inquiry which will give him understanding of what others have done by way of understanding the whale, and the cetology he rehearses is added to this as an attempt to decode the creature in "some systematized exhibition of the whale in his broad genera" by citing what "the best and latest authorities have laid down" (ch. 32). All of these forms of scientific inquiry—linguistic, bibliographical, and naturalist—are finally failures, "the classification of the constituents of a chaos," and he must finally own, with one of the authorities he quotes, that there is an " 'impenetrable veil covering our knowledge of the cetacea' " (ch. 32). These intellectual, academic assaults on the whale, however, come "ere the Pequod's weedy hull rolls side by side with the barnacled hulls of the leviathan" (ch. 32). Before the direct encounter with any whale, before "the first lowering" (ch. 48), Ishmael is introduced to the idea of the whale of whales, Moby-Dick, the figurement of which will finally present to him the paradigmatic symbol of the created order. He is pulled toward the moment of this presentation, and for the response to that moment, all his "whale-hunting"—all his inquiries into the whale—will prepare him.

From the moment of his encounter with the "marvellous painting" in which the whale presents itself to him as the paramount figurement of the wonder-world, and especially after "the first lowering" which is "a sight full of quick wonder and awe" (ch. 48), Ishmael attempts to survey the whale and all—the spirit-spout, the doubloon, the ambergris, the brit—that seems to refer to it. He inquires into the "monstrous pictures of whales" (ch. 55), into the "less erroneous pictures of whales" (ch. 56), and into what seem to his sense of things to be "the true pictures of whaling scenes" (ch. 56). He assays "whales in paint; in teeth; in wood; in sheet-iron; in stone; in mountains; in stars" (ch. 57). Each of these attempts, however, takes him away from the whale—into folklore, into scholarship, into art, into astrology—in the sense at least that, with these methods, he cannot front the whale in its proper element, the great seas of life. And, thus, he begins more fully to employ his senses in his grappling with the idea of the whale as he discusses "the whale as a dish" (ch. 65) for Stubb and for the sharks (ch. 66). Finally, he turns his attention to the whale proper with discussion of "that not unvexed subject, the skin of the whale" (ch. 68), the Sphynx-like head of the whale (ch. 70), in its contrasted views and double vision (chs. 74 and 75). In these discussions, Ishmael plies the methods of physiology, and in succeeding chapters (77–80) in which he explores the face, skull, and brain of the whale, he employs the phrenological method which requires a figurative neural and spinal surgery. As the course of the narrative journey continues, Ishmael successively seeks to "dissect"

the whale in order to uncover the source of his spouting—"the fountain"—
in the "remarkable involved Cretan labyrinth" (ch. 85) of the heart and
lungs and in order to explain "the sole means of propulsion"—"the tail"—
and the "great motions . . . peculiar to it" (ch. 86). When he turns to the
life and habits of the whale, Ishmael involves himself in dissertations on
"leviathan amours" (ch. 87), the social covenant of the whale (ch. 87), the
whale as "school-master" (ch. 88), the cultural condition of the whale in
the face of the whaling industry (chs. 89 and 90), the social uses of the
whale's ambergris, "a very curious substance" (ch. 92), the sperm, "that
inexpressible sperm" (ch. 94), and the more frivolous uses of the whale's
penis (ch. 95). Having "chiefly dwelt upon the marvels of his outer aspect
. . . [or] upon some few interior structural features," Ishmael has the op-
portunity in "a bower in the Arsacides" to study the whale "in his ultimatum; that is to say, in his unconditional skeleton" (ch. 102), and there
he attempts a "measurement of the whale's skeleton" (ch. 103). The ana-
tomical research of the bones of the whale leads Ishmael, in turn, to consider
the geological remains of "the fossil whale" (ch. 104), which themselves
force him to ponder the generation of the whale species. "Does the whale
diminish?" Ishmael asks himself; "will he perish?" (ch. 105). He has seen
"the dying whale" (ch. 116), but the generic whale, Ishmael must conclude,
must be considered "immortal in his species, however perishable in his
individuality" (ch. 105): "this Leviathan comes floundering down upon us
from the headwaters of the Eternities" and "the eternal whale will still
survive" (ch. 105) when the generations of man have passed. Utilizing
every method at its disposal, then, Ishmael's rationality has inquired into
the whale's external and internal aspect and has followed the whale from
birth in "The Grand Armada" to his "perishable individuality" in "The
Dying Whale." He has aimed at a "thorough sweeping comprehension"
(ch. 102) of the whale; and it is perhaps no accident that the chapter at the
very center of the book is entitled "Cutting in" (ch. 67). But for all his
rational inquiry, Ishmael finally reaches the non-rational conclusion that
the whale is eternal, that it cannot be fathomed by reason, that he cannot
"contain" the whale.

The conclusion of his rational inquiries—the discovery by way of his
reasoning of the limits of reason—is not the end of the matter, for, con-
current with his more or less systematic and analytical inquiries into the
whale, Ishmael has developed a progressive imagination of the whale as
the paradigmatic element of the wonder-world to which the transcendent
is episodically and symbolically present. In virtually every rational encounter with the whale, Ishmael finds in it that which is allusive of a
dimension overreaching its concrete and palpable form and yet adhering to

that form. In this portentousness both the revelation and the concealment, the high speech and inestimable silence, belong to the manifestation of the holy. In these manifestations Ishmael recognizes that which, if it cannot be contained, cannot at all be refused in its implications for his life. As he and Queequeg "were mildly employed weaving what is called a sword-mat" and as Ishmael finds the workings of this "Loom of Time" (ch. 47) a source for his metaphysical speculations, as it implies the interweaving of necessity and free will, the entire speculation must be dropped because of the cry of the whale. The moment of the first lowering—of Ishmael's first direct encounter with the whale—surpasses all else in its demand as symbol. The ultimatum of the whale is that of direct encounter, not of perusing his "unconditional skeleton." After he has measured the skeleton of the whale, Ishmael has owned: "How vain and foolish, then, thought I, for timid untravelled man to try to comprehend aright this wondrous whale, by merely poring over his dead attenuated skeleton, stretched in this peaceful wood. No. Only in the heart of quickest perils; only when within the eddyings of his angry flukes; only on the profound unbounded sea, can the fully invested whale be truly and livingly found out" (ch. 103). Having vowed in the third chapter to "find out" the whale, then, Ishmael must take the span of the whale's portentousness by swimming " 'Twixt the whale's black flukes." The wonder of the whale has awakened in Ishmael surmise as to its origin, and it is to the origin of its symbolic figurement that he wants to trace it.

From his first direct fronting of the whale in his proper element, however, Ishmael begins to suspect that, scientific inquiry having everywhere brought him to the conclusion that the whale is allusive of the eternal, he must approach the whale with eyes prepared for the whale's inherent symbolism. He must develop a special sort of vision:

> To a landsman, no whale, nor any sign of a herring, would have been visible at that moment; nothing but a troubled bit of greenish white water, and thin scattered puffs of vapor hovering over it, and suffusingly blowing off to leeward, like the confused scud from white rolling billows. The air around suddenly vibrated and tingled, as it were, like the air over intensely heated plates of iron. Beneath this atmospheric waving and curling, and partially beneath a thin layer of water, also, the whales were swimming. Seen in advance of all the other indications, the puffs of vapor they spouted, seemed their forerunning couriers and detached flying outriders.
>
> (ch. 48)

Here, during "The First Lowering," Ishmael's initial encounter with the whale in the midst of "the profound unbounded sea" presents him with the elusiveness of the whale and with the hazardous aspect of "the vast swells of the omnipotent sea" (ch. 48). After this beginning, with all its luminous atmosphere which "vibrated and tingled," he confirms that the whale inhabits the center of the wonder-world within which he must ply reasons of the heart: "Not the raw recruit, marching from the bosom of his wife into the fever heat of his first battle; not the dead man's ghost encountering the first unknown phantom of the other world;—neither of these can feel stranger and stronger emotions than that man does, who for the first time finds himself pulling into the charmed, churned circle of the hunted sperm whale" (ch. 48). In the course of the narrative which follows from this first encounter, the whale will intermittently present to Ishmael moments to be encountered as *kairos* and symbol, and the nascent responses to the whale which he experiences in this, his first, encounter will grow until his recovery of the transcendent is complete.

In each encounter with the whale, Ishmael recognizes, after the assays of rational inquiry have run their course, that the whale, the singular grand analogue, the wonder-world itself, portends the transcendent. When he contemplates "The Great Heidelberg Tun of the Sperm Whale," he sees that "as that famous great tierce is mystically carved in front, so the whale's vast plaited forehead forms innumerable strange devices for the emblematical adornment of the whale's fluids." The great tun becomes, for Ishmael, "the secret inner chamber or sanctum sanctorum of the whale" (ch. 78). When he muses on the spouting of the whale—his fountain—Ishmael again finds the presaging aspect which brims over with the presence of the transcendent:

> And how nobly it raises our conceit of the mighty, misty monster, to behold him solemnly sailing through a calm tropical sea; his vast, mild head overhung by a canopy of vapor, engendered by his incommunicable contemplations, and that vapor—as you will sometimes see it—glorified by a rainbow, as if Heaven itself had put its seal upon his thoughts. For, d'ye see, rainbows do not visit the clear air; they only irradiate vapor. And so, through all the thick mists of the dim doubts in my mind, divine intuitions now and then shoot, enkindling my fog with a heavenly ray. And for this I thank God; for all have doubts; many deny; but doubts or denials, few along with them, have intuitions. Doubts of all things earthly, and intuitions of some things heav-

enly; this combination makes neither believer nor infidel, but makes a man who regards them both with equal eye.

(ch. 85)

He continues to develop his "intuitions of some things heavenly" when he encounters both the "graceful flexion" and the "Titanism of Power" which are disclosed in the whale's mighty tail:

Excepting the sublime *breach*—somewhere else to be described— this peaking of the whale's flukes is perhaps the grandest sight to be seen in all animated nature. Out of the bottomless pro- fundities the gigantic tail seems spasmodically snatching at the highest heaven. So in dreams, have I seen majestic Satan thrust- ing forth his tormented colossal claw from the flame Baltic of Hell. But in gazing at such scenes, it is all in all what mood you are in; if in the Dantean, the devils will occur to you; if in that of Isaiah, the arch-angels. Standing at the mast-head of my ship during a sunrise that crimsoned sky and sea, I once saw a large herd of whales in the east, all heading towards the sun, and for a moment vibrating in concert with peaked flukes As it seemed to me at the time, such a grand embodiment of adoration of the gods was never beheld, even in Persia, in the home of the fire worshippers.

(ch. 86)

In these and other instances, then, Ishmael discovers the uncanny revelations of the wholly other in his experience, for the symbolic vestigium of the whale gives off mystic references, transcendent allusions, signals of another world. The whale is revelatory, and Ishmael has eyes for such a symbol, instinct with significance. As a singular symbol of the wonder-world, the whale, like that unfettered and charged world, signals the hand of the creator, as Ishmael suggests after his scrutiny of the "sublime" brow of the whale:

Few are the foreheads which like Shakspeare's [sic] or Melanc- thon's rise so high, and descend so low, that the eyes themselves seem clear, eternal, tideless mountain lakes; and all above them in the forehead's wrinkles, you seem to track the antlered thoughts descending there to drink, as the Highland hunters track the snow prints of the deer. But in the great Sperm Whale, this high and mighty god-like dignity inherent in the brow is so immensely amplified, that gazing on it, in that full front view, you feel the Deity and the dread powers more forcibly than in beholding any other object in living nature. For you see no one point precisely; not one distinct feature is revealed; no nose, eyes, ears, or mouth; no face; he has none, proper; nothing but that one broad firmament of a forehead, pleated with riddles.

(ch. 79)

If in profile the forehead's "grandeur does not domineer upon you so," nor "does this wondrous brow diminish" (ch. 79). When fronted, however, this "mystical brow," for Ishmael, "signifies—'God: done this day by my hand'" (ch. 79). Bearing the signature of the transcendent, then, the world is revelatory: it contains, and discloses, in the midst of the world of human experience, the momentary but continuing portentousness of the ground of all experience in and through what Carlyle called "the wondrous agency of symbols."

If the whale reveals as a symbol, however, it also conceals as a symbol; the concrete realm may present signals of the presence of the wholly other but such signals—looming through finite forms—can never fully manifest the transcendent, as Ishmael learns in his reflections on the symbolism of the whale. The "Heidelberg Tun" of the whale might present to his contemplations a mystical and emblematic aspect, but the interiority of the whale's tun—its "sanctum sanctorum" (ch. 78)—can only be entered, as in the case of Tashtego's falling there, at the risk of perishing. The fountain of the whale, revelatory as it is in "enkindling my fog with a heavenly ray," presents, finally, only "incommunicable contemplations"—a vapor which recedes almost at the moment of its appearance (ch. 85): "And as for this whale's spout," he must finally allow, "you might almost stand in it, and yet be undecided as to what it is precisely" (ch. 85). Again, although the whale's tail discloses itself in gestures "snatching at the highest heaven," Ishmael cannot explain its meaning:

The more I consider this mighty tail, the more do I deplore my inability to express it. At times there are gestures in it, which, though they would well grace the hand of man, remain wholly inexplicable. In an extensive herd, so remarkable, occasionally, are these mystic gestures, that I have heard hunters who have declared them akin to Free-Mason signs and symbols; that the whale, indeed, by these methods intelligently conversed with the world. Nor are there wanting other motions of the whale in his general body, full of strangeness, and unaccountable to his most experienced assailant. Dissect him how I may, then, I but go skin deep; I know him not, and never will. But if I know

> not even the tail of this whale, how understand his head? much more, how comprehend his face, when face he has none? Thou shalt see my back parts, my tail, he seems to say, but my face shall not be seen. But I cannot completely make out his back parts; and hint what he will about his face, I say again he has no face.
>
> (ch. 86)

Unable to "dissect" the tail completely in order to fathom the ultimate meaning of its disclosures, he cannot either "read" the final character and motive of the whale's brow. Although that brow signifies God, Ishmael's attempts to contain it are failures: "for you see no point precisely; not one distinct feature is revealed; no nose, eyes, ears, or mouth; no face; he has none, proper; nothing but that one broad firmament of a forehead, pleated with riddles" (ch. 79). Without obtaining an answer, he is left with a rhetorical question—"how may unlettered Ishmael hope to read the awful Chaldee of the Sperm Whale's brow?" (ch. 79)—the answer to which is that no amount of tutoring will enable such a reading. The whale does not appear to him after the images of the human; it has no face which will mirror back a recognizable and apprehensible form: it comes to Ishmael, rather, only as a "broad firmament"—as that which is nonhuman and which presents the wholly other in its dense and opaque and finally furtive reality. Ishmael's encounter with the hidden God is strongly reminiscent of the poem by Emily Dickinson beginning "My period had come for Prayer" (c. 1862) as the persona finds that her artful "tactics" of prayer fail to recover for her the "Creator." She searches for this rudiment among the domestic images familiar to her—a house, a chimney, a door—only to find herself confronted with "Vast Prairies of Air / Unbroken by a Settler" which are equivalent to the "broad firmament" Ishmael finds on the whale's brow. Just as Ishmael declares then that the whale "has no face," the persona of the Dickinson poem asks "Infinitude—Had'st Thou no Face/That I might look on Thee?" Finally, she discovers in the midst of the vast, silent creation that she is "awed beyond my errand" and that she "worshipped—did not 'pray.' " Ishmael, too, will learn that in the "Afric Temple of the Whale" his tactics are not sufficient. Although the whale portends the presence of the transcendent, it also leaves Ishmael with the intractable reality of the hidden transcendent.

III

Understood in this way, then, Ishmael follows a course of inquiry with respect to the whale—and the mysterious world it symbolizes—which fi-

nally ends without his having penetrated to its final meaning. He begins
with a rationality which seeks a "thorough and sweeping comprehension"
(ch. 102) of the whale, but this form of inquiry fails him when it broaches
on the whale as symbol. He then plies the reasons of the heart to find the
truth of the symbols, but this method also fails him, for although he locates
revelation in symbols he discovers concealment as well. The whale might
allude, in abundant moments, to the transcendent, but the allusion is finally
a riddle which hides its transcendent source:

> In life, the visible surface of the Sperm Whale is not the least
> among the many marvels he presents. Almost invariably it is all
> over obliquely crossed and re-crossed with numberless straight
> marks in thick array, something like those in the finest Italian
> line engravings. But these marks do not seem to be impressed
> upon the isinglass substance above mentioned, but seem to be
> seen through it, as if they were engraved on the body itself. Nor
> is this all. In some instances, to the quick, observant eye, those
> linear marks, as in a veritable engraving, but afford the ground
> for far other delineations. These are hieroglyphical; that is, if
> you call those mysterious cyphers on the walls of pyramids
> hieroglyphics, then that is the proper word to use in the present
> connexion. By my retentive memory of the hieroglyphics upon
> one Sperm Whale in particular, I was much struck with a plate
> representing the old Indian characters chiselled on the famous
> hieroglyphic palisades on the banks of the Upper Mississippi.
> Like those mystic rocks, too, the mystic-marked whale remains
> undecipherable.
>
> (ch. 68)

Inquire how he will—by way of rationality or by way of the imagination
of symbol—Ishmael's inquiries end in, are prevented by, the opaque character of the symbols themselves: he is left facing the hieroglyphic whale—
the riddle of the wonder-world—with all its immense and fecund, but finally
clouded, presentations of itself. He can front the whale, but what he finds
there are the "mysterious cyphers" of a transcendent presence. He has
confirmed what he had earlier suspected:

> For all these reasons, then, any way you may look at it, you
> must needs conclude that the great Leviathan is that one creature
> in the world which must remain unpainted to the last. True,
> one portrait may hit the mark much nearer than another, but

none can hit it with any very considerable degree of exactness. So there is no earthly way of finding out precisely what the whale really looks like. And the only mode in which you can derive even a tolerable idea of his living contour, is by going a whaling yourself; but by so doing, you run no small risk of being eternally stove and sunk by him. Wherefore, it seems to me you had best not be too fastidious in your curiosity touching this Leviathan.

(ch. 55)

These reflections suggest both the necessity of the direct encounter with the marvelous aspect of the whale and the idea of the dread power of the whale as a portent of the transcendent which retains the *mysterium* and *tremendum* belonging to the wholly other. Since the whale figures forth the created order itself, Ishmael has learned that he must acknowledge the radical otherness of the transcendent dimension which looms up in his experience, must admit finally that the ground of experience will "remain unpainted to the last." A portrait of the whale is impossible because "I say again he has no face" (ch. 86).

The reasons of the heart do not end here, however, for, despite the ambiguity of the whale's revelations and despite Ishmael's inability to penetrate to the final character of the transcendent ground of the wonder-world, he has touched upon the dimension of ultimacy in his experience and in this has recovered the sense of the transcendent which animated his searching. What was at stake for him, from the outset, was not the solution to the final character and motive of the transcendent. What he sought, rather, was the truth of the human heart, and he bottoms upon that truth only after he has traced his initial wonderment to its source and, there, has encountered the whale which signifies God. After touching on the source of wonder, even if he cannot decode its riddles, he returns to the world to find wonder manifest everywhere. And this is the meaning of the transcendent for Ishmael: although he cannot fully know the transcendent, he knows that it enables his self-transcendence by presenting him with a world brimming with spiritual resonance, a world touched by wonder, a world containing the possibility for him to conceive his life within the mixed shades and shadows of ultimacy. The epistemological dilemma he confronts in the whale does not end in despair: if there is concealment, there is revelation. The issue of knowing, rather, returns him, by the reasons of the heart, to the world of the human, redeemed by wonder. In attempting to seize the precious fluids of the whale, he receives "a squeeze of the hand":

I squeezed that sperm till a strange sort of insanity came over me; and I found myself unwittingly squeezing my co-laborers' hands in it, mistaking their hands for the gentle globules. Such an abounding, affectionate, friendly, loving feeling did this avocation beget; that at last I was continually squeezing their hands, and looking up into their eyes sentimentally; as much as to say,— Oh! my dear fellow beings, why should we longer cherish any social acerbities, or know the slightest ill-humor or envy! Come; let us squeeze hands all round; nay, let us all squeeze ourselves into each other; let us squeeze ourselves universally into the very milk and sperm of kindness.

Would that I could keep squeezing that sperm for ever! For now, since by many prolonged, repeated experiences, I have perceived that in all cases man must eventually lower, or at least shift, his conceit of attainable felicity; not placing it anywhere in the intellect or the fancy; but in the wife, the heart, the bed, the table, the saddle, the fire-side, the country; now that I have perceived all this, I am ready to squeeze case eternally. In visions of the night, I saw long rows of angels in paradise, each with his hands in a jar of spermaceti.

(ch. 94)

If his "attainable felicity" had been centered for a time around the final explication of the character and meaning of the transcendent, if he has craved that truth, Ishmael has proved that he craves the human even more. His epistemological dilemma in the face of the inviolably hidden transcendent reaches its denouement in his reconciliation with the world of his living. Had he not undertaken his inquiries and had he not encountered the real presence of the hidden God, he might have returned to the world of "the table, the saddle, the fire-side" without any sense of its wonder. Having discovered such a presence, he can find all his experience charged and resonant and instinct with significance.

The shift of "his conceit of attainable felicity," then, represents to Ishmael not an end in despair but a beginning in piety. He has encountered the whale which stands symbolically at the center of the creation, and he has seen that, although the whale and the creation must remain unsolved to the last, the creation is plenteous, that it contains those radiant moments, abundant with spirit, which are redemptive. As a figure for the wonder-world, with its transcendent allusiveness and profundity, the whale evokes from Ishmael a *sursum corda*; after attempting to measure the whale, after the failure to decipher its hieroglyph, and after "the squeeze of the hand," he encounters "the fossil whale"—the whale as old as the earth, built into and preserved in the very terrain of the earth—and "in this Afric Temple of the Whale I leave you, reader, and if you be a Nantucketer, and a whaleman, you will silently worship there" (ch. 104).

Thus, in the figure and career of Ishmael, Melville plots the integral response to a world freighted with significances of a spiritual presence, and this response issues in the deepest kind of reconciliation with the terms of experience. Ishmael had been committed, from early in his questing, to seek out an exhilarated world and to explore its resonances in relation to the tangled web at the center of his own heart. The final implications of his humanity, he senses, can only be settled in the context of, and in an authentic response to, that encompassing symbolic world which rises up around him. In the process implied by taking the span of portents—that is, in the process of expecting a full-freighted world, of discovering in it portents of a transcendent dimension, of scrutinizing the contours of these portents, and of possessing their significance for his life—Ishmael learns of the last complications of human life, learns of the revelatory, but ultimately opaque, character of life in history, and learns that his mortal condition derives its own significance only in an integral response to the immense mystery which is intermittently present to him.

Moby-Dick, An American Lyrical Novel

Bert Bender

> *"Dissect him how I may, then, I but go skin deep; I know him not, and never will."*
>
> Ishmael

Among the countless critical efforts to "know" *Moby-Dick*, those that have lanced closest to "the innermost life of the fish" have praised its deep poetic nature. These tributes range from Alfred Kazin's description of the novel's "poetic power" and Richard Chase's praise of "Melville the unsurpassable poet" to F. O. Matthiessen's more technical analysis of the Shakespearean influence on *Moby-Dick*'s language. There is no question that *Moby-Dick* contains some of America's most impressive poetry. Yet there is still plenty of sea room in which to pursue the book's elusive but truly poetic nature as a whole. My proposition is that the best way to catch sight of *Moby-Dick*'s poetic wholeness is to approach it as a kind of lyrical novel whose form and organization derive from the psychological attitude Melville assumed in struggling to compose it.

Moby-Dick's essential lyricism is not fully appreciable simply through analysis of the technically "poetic" qualities of its language—e.g., its richness of rhythm, sound, or imagery: "lyric" and "poetic" are slippery and scarcely synonymous terms. And while most of the qualities that are now frequently associated with the lyric genre are to be found in *Moby-Dick* ("brevity, metrical coherence, subjectivity, passion, sensuality, and particularity of image"), its lyricism is most deeply related to the origins of the

From *Studies in the Novel* 10, no. 3 (Fall 1978). © 1978 by North Texas State University.

lyric mode in ancient religious practices and to contemporary definitions of genres that focus on the artist's attitude toward his creation. According to such definitions, James Joyce, for example, sees the lyric as a personal utterance; Northrop Frye, in defining genres according to "the radical of presentation," sees the lyric as a form in which the poet turns his back on his audience and pretends "to be talking to someone else: a spirit of nature, a Muse . . . , a personal friend, a lover, a god, a personified abstraction, or a natural object"; and, more precisely to my point here, André Gide defines "lyricism as a state in which man allows himself to surrender to God." *Moby-Dick* is obviously so protean as to defy absolute classification, but in its wholeness it comes to us most deeply as a religious lyric in which Melville finds and surrenders to his "God."

A theory of *The Lyrical Novel* has been provided, of course, by Ralph Freedman, who briefly mentions *Moby-Dick* as an example of the genre. But, while Freedman's theory provides a general basis for discerning the nature of lyrical fiction, it is concerned with European and British literary traditions (offering detailed studies of Hesse, Gide, and Woolf), and does not adequately (because it does not intend to) account for the peculiar lyrical quality of *Moby-Dick*. According to Freedman, the essence of lyrical narrative is "a mood, a type of literary sensibility, a way of approaching knowledge," all of which is manifested in a particular work when "the world is reduced to *a* lyrical point of view, the equivalent of the poet's 'I': the lyrical self." This much of *The Lyrical Novel* helps explain the dynamics of *Moby-Dick*; but, devoted as it is to studies of Hesse, Gide, and Woolf, Freedman's analysis emphasizes formal aesthetics and techniques which do not characterize Melville. The "techniques" and "poetic effects" of the lyrical writers discussed by Freedman result in the transformation of their perceptions into "networks of images" or "designs" or "patterns of imagery," in short, "portraiture, the halting of the flow of time within constellations of images or figures." But the lyrical techniques of Hesse, Gide, and Woolf (as described by Freedman) are as foreign to Melville as his sensibility is to theirs. Thus, while the authors of *Moby-Dick* and, for example, *The Waves* might share a mood or "way of approaching knowledge" that is generally lyrical, a good deal remains to be said about how *Moby-Dick*'s lyricism is uniquely Melvillean and American.

The critical debate that tends to see either Ahab or Ishmael as the book's dominating consciousness has obscured what Freedman would call the lyrical "I" or the poet's (Melville's) mask in *Moby-Dick*. First Ahab and then, more recently, Ishmael have been taken as the dominating force in *Moby-Dick*; and, partly because Ahab and Ishmael are so different, many have concluded that the book as a whole lacks resolution. C. Hugh Holman, for example, has written that the book's "major weakness" is that "Ahab's story was Shakespearean and Ishmael's Dantesque"; the "imperfect fusion" of these "two elements" results from "Melville's having written the book on two different levels at two different times" and from his "ignorance of the importance of precisely defining the relation of the narrator to the story he narrates." A more helpful analysis of the Ishmael/Ahab struggle is provided by Charles Feidelson, who feels that Ishmael is more than a mere "surrogate for an absentee author" but Melville's *Doppelgänger,* as well. But Feidelson concludes that the "obvious dilemma" in *Moby-Dick* is not resolved because "Melville has not resolved it for himself": Melville "discovers that he is potentially an Ahab, the devil's partisan, the nihilist," as well as an Ishmael, "the voyaging mind, the capacity for vision."

My own interpretation of this dilemma is that, both before and after the composition of *Moby-Dick,* Melville struggled with the conflicting moods that he dramatized in 1850–51 as Ishmael and Ahab. Melville was neither Ahab nor Ishmael, simply, as we see in his famous letters to Hawthorne during this period, where both moods are evident. In *Moby-Dick* he managed momentarily to resolve this conflict in the same way that John Donne could temporarily resolve his own inner conflict in the Holy Sonnets—by dramatizing a colloquy between his conflicting selves within a single piece. Obviously, *Moby-Dick* and Donne's Holy Sonnets are more than just centuries apart; my comparison is intended to show only that in each we see the projected inner drama of the author's struggle to subdue his doubt and maintain his faith. In each case, the doubting or diabolic self is fully admitted into the dramatized struggle in order that it can be subdued at least momentarily. Thus Melville brings to life and dramatizes the full force of Ahab in order to purge it from himself; and Donne, in "Death Be Not Proud," for example, addresses "Death" directly in order that it be defeated within the meditation, which ends, "Death thou shalt die"; or he can, within other sonnets, affirm that, "to vex me, contraryes meete in one," or that "black sinne hath betraid to endlesse night / My worlds both parts,"—only to imagine a cessation: "To morrow I quake with true feare of his rod," or "burne me ô Lord, with a fiery zeale."

The psychology of creation involved in *Moby-Dick* and the Holy Sonnets is certainly more complex than the description I offer here, which is meant to comprehend the creative process on only one level. Other related but deeper and more complex psychological forces at work in *Moby-Dick* have been described in many famous Freudian and Jungian interpretations. But my purpose here is to argue that the dramatized resolution of conflicting selves is part of the religious attitude assumed by Melville in composing *Moby-Dick*, and that this attitude determines its genre—a kind of lyrical novel in which Melville "allows himself to surrender to God." It would be foolish to insist that *Moby-Dick* is nothing but a lyrical novel, but in this religious sense it is akin to the lyrical genre which, as Frye has suggested, "is to *epos*, rhetorically, as prayer is to sermon. The radical of presentation in the lyric is the hypothetical form of what in religion is called the 'I-Thou' relationship." But the question is, how does this all work in *Moby-Dick*; what is the nature of Melville's "God"; and where can he be seen surrendering to this "God"?

That Melville was powerfully influenced by the Bible and that he believed in "God," there is no doubt; nor is there any doubt that his attitude toward Christianity and his concept of God fluctuated with his moods throughout his life. His religious meditations were far too restless, complex, and doubt-ridden to allow fixed belief in anything (particularly in any institution or dogma), or our efforts to systematize them. As Hawthorne wrote of him (after their visit in Liverpool, where Melville had stopped on his way to the Holy Land in 1856), "He can neither believe, nor be comfortable in his unbelief; and he is too honest and courageous not to try to do one or the other." But his struggle with belief and his fluctuating attitudes toward "God" are due largely to the options that his culture made available to him, i.e., to particular definitions of the nature of God. If he was an "Accuser of the Deity," as William Braswell has argued, it is in the sense that he denied the Christian concept of a "wholly benevolent deity"; and if he can be said to have "hated" God, as Lawrence Thompson has argued, it was for similar reasons. Melville's main quarrel was not with God but with particular definitions of God. Certainly, this is the sense of his remark to Hawthorne: "Yes, that word [God] is the hangman. Take God out of the dictionary, and you would have Him in the street." Indeed, the most compelling attribute of Melville's God is His ambiguousness, even more than His terrifying power. For, as Nathalia Wright has concluded in *Melville's Use of the Bible*, he may be considered to have shared "the great tragic tradition of the Hebrews, who regarded the creation, for all its mystery and terror, as the garment of Jehovah." Like the Hebrews, for whom "this world was vague," Melville believed that "the primal truth" was represented not by "order, rhetoric, and logic," but by "elemental and undisciplined energy."

We are therefore allowed only glimpses of Melville's "God" as he is imagined in various guises throughout the book—e.g., the Old Testament God invoked by Father Mapple; the "great democratic God" (invoked in

"Knights and Squires"); the tolerator of voracious sharkishness (as in "Stubb's Supper" and "The Whale as a Dish"); the pagan "Yojo" through whom Queequeg "gave up his life into the hands of his gods" (in "The Monkey-Rope"); "the seductive god . . . Pan" (in "The Pacific"); or the ubiquitous Moby-Dick himself. But these accumulated glimpses are subsumed in a Godhead who, as in Isaiah, could declare, "I form the light, and create darkness: I make peace, and create evil: I the LORD do all these *things*" (Isa. 45:7. In *Moby-Dick* the presence of this kind of vague and dreadful God is explicit in passages where Melville addresses "God." And such a presence is implied throughout the book in general by Melville's Biblical language; his countless direct and indirect references to the Old Testament; his cast of such Old Testament names as Ishmael, Jonah, Job, or Ahab; and by the almost complete omission of any mention of Christ, who had figured so strongly in *White-Jacket* (1850) and in whose image Melville cast Hawthorne in "Hawthorne and His Mosses" (1850). Further, the pervasive presence of a vague and awesome Godhead—the creator of light *and* dark—is the source of one of *Moby-Dick*'s deepest aesthetic principles: its sense of balance. The contrasting but complementary personalities of Ishmael and Ahab; the imaged balance in "The Mast-head," "A Right Whale Killed" (the *Pequod* regaining "her even keel" by counterpoising the hoisted sperm whale's head with that of the right whale—Kant balancing out Locke), and "The Monkey-Rope" (the civilized Ishmael again wedded with the primitive Queequeg); and the image of the Catskill Eagle diving and soaring: these are the products of a mind that, in projecting a sublimely balanced creation, can balance within itself "doubts of all things earthly, and intuitions of some things heavenly." But finally, a vague, all-encompassing God is present in *Moby-Dick* as the cause of the book's innumerable lyric flights, its wondering meditations on the sea and the soul, and death. In such lyric passages, as Gide might have remarked, Melville surrenders to his God, at once resolving his own inner conflict and realizing the means of Ishmael's survival.

These lyric passages comprise a large part of *Moby-Dick*, and many have been quoted at length by critics like Richard Chase in his tribute to Melville's "incomparable discoveries of language." Often, they exist as small chapters characterized by a "wavelike amplification and building-up, followed by the lyric subsidence at the end." One recalls, for example, the chapter "Nantucket," which sings "in Bible language" of the heroic Nantucketers, conquerors of the "watery world," and builds toward its quotable end: "With the landless gull, that at sunset folds her wings and is rocked to sleep between billows; so at nightfall, the Nantucketer, out of sight of land, furls his sails, and lays him to his rest, while under his very pillow rush herds of walruses and whales." And—to recall just a few more—there are memorable lyric passages in such chapters as "The Lee Shore," a commemoration of Bulkington's "ocean-perishing" and a celebration of the sea, where "alone resides the highest truth, shoreless, indefinite as God"; or "Knights and Squires," with its memorable tribute to "that democratic dignity which, on all hands, radiates without end from God; Himself! The great God absolute!"; or "The Mast-head," which depicts the mast-head's dreamy, dangerous loss of identity as, swayed aloft by "the inscrutable tides of God," he "takes the mystic ocean at his feet for the visible image of that deep, blue, bottomless soul, prevading mankind and nature"; or in such other chapters as "The Whiteness of the Whale," "Brit," "The Fountain," "The Grand Armada," "The Castaway," "A Squeeze of the Hand," "The Pacific," "The Blacksmith," and "The Gilder."

In these passages Melville confronts some thought or natural phenomenon which he finds rationally impenetrable and which elicits his characteristic response of lyric wonder. Thus, while he may begin such a passage by bidding us to "consider" a particular phenomenon, he ends in a lyric, awe-struck expression of wonder or amazement, a surrender to an unfathomable God whose presence he affirms. Confronted with the blank fact of whiteness, for example, he knows that "to analyze it, would seem impossible," for, among other things, it is "the very veil of the Christian's Deity." His response to the first albatross he ever saw is a model of this kind of experience: "At intervals, it arched forth its vast archangel wings, as if to embrace some holy ark. Wondrous flutterings and throbbings shook it. . . . As Abraham before the angels, I bowed myself." Or, again, contemplating similarly amazing phenomena, his response is to exclaim, "what are the comprehensible terrors of man compared with the interlinked terrors and wonders of God!" *Moby-Dick*'s ultimate values are evident in these submissive lyric responses: the wondrous creation that they acknowledge, and the very capacity to *have* such responses—to make such gestures of faith. Decidedly, these are not Ahab's values, of whom Stubb said, " 'I never yet saw him kneel,' " but they give *Moby-Dick* its orientation, its sense of balance.

The posture of reverence and submission implies a kind of faith that many readers of Melville will not accept. But, always a pressing subject for Melville, the question of faith or confidence exists at the very heart of *Moby-Dick* in a way that distinguishes Melville's mood of 1850–51 from that darker one of 1857, for example, when he published *The Confidence-Man*. It is appropriate in *Moby-Dick* that Ishmael raises the question of faith in "The Chapel," where, contemplating the marble tablets that honored lost whaling men, he is moved to one of his first extended lyric expressions:

> Oh! ye whose dead lie buried beneath the green grasses; who standing among flowers can say—here, *here* lies my beloved; ye know not the desolation that broods in bosoms like these. What bitter blanks in those black-bordered marbles which cover no ashes! What despair in those immovable inscriptions! What deadly voids and unbidden infidelities in the lines that seem to gnaw upon all Faith, and refuse resurrections to the beings who have placelessly perished without a grave. As well might those tablets stand in the cave of Elephanta as here.

But, midway through this meditation, Ishmael turns from seeing Faith as gnawed upon by the fact of death to assert that "Faith, like a jackal, feeds among the tombs, and even from these dead doubts she gathers her most vital hope." Then, admitting that "there is death in this business of whaling—a speechlessly quick chaotic bundling of a man into Eternity," he goes on to think that "we have hugely mistaken this matter of Life and Death. . . . [W]hat they call my shadow here on earth is my true substance." "Therefore," he concludes, "come a stove boat and stove body when they will, for stave my soul, Jove himself cannot."

Exuberant as such moments are, it should be clear that Ishmael's is scarcely a blind faith. He maintains it with a certain willfulness, as Starbuck does when gazing into the sea: " 'Loveliness unfathomable, as ever lover saw in his young bride's eye!—Tell me not of thy teeth-tiered sharks, and thy kidnapping cannibal ways. Let faith oust fact; let fancy oust memory; I look deep down and do believe.' " The key to Ishmael's faith is that, while he has his doubts along with his divine intuitions, he can sense the inadequacy of reason and willfully suspend his doubts. This spiritual sense of balance distinguishes him from Ahab, whose willfully inverted faith *is* blind. Ahab finds only "tarnished" treasure when he gazes into the same sea that inspired Starbuck to affirm his faith; and, later, he mocks the carpenter (at work on Ishmael's means of salvation, the life-buoy coffin): " 'Faith? What's that?' " Ishmael's opposite, Ahab willfully denies any "intuitions of things heavenly" and therefore has nothing to balance his own "prouder, if . . . darker faith."

The question of faith, then, deeply underlies this whole book, but the form it takes is best characterized by the term "wonder." Perhaps because of its inherent complexity, "wonder" became one of Melville's favorite words in *Moby-Dick*. While it indicates something not only marvellous or surprising, but perhaps supernatural or miraculous, it also carries the sense, as a verb, "to think" or "to doubt." In *Moby-Dick* Melville uses the word in its fullest sense, indicating a state or mood in which analytical thought or doubt are suspended even though they are present beneath the surface. Thus, his meditations lead him repeatedly to the threshold of wonder, where he suspends reason in surrendering to his unreasonable God. Indeed, the entrance to *Moby-Dick* is accomplished in this way: having decided to see the "watery part of the world," Ishmael begins to think of the magic in water and concludes that the key to it all is that rivers and oceans contain "the image of the ungraspable-phantom of life." Thus, the prelude "Loomings" ends: "the great flood-gates of the wonder-world swung open, and in the wild conceits that swayed me to my purpose, two and two there floated into my inmost soul, endless processions of the whale, and midmost of them all, one grand hooded phantom, like a snow hill in the air."

The capacity for lyric wonder and faith resides mainly within Ishmael, and it is the essential criterion by which Melville establishes his values and distinguishes between wisdom and madness. Ahab is himself no mean poet, but for all his grand style, he lacks Ishmael's consoling sense of wonder. Melville makes this crucial distinction in "The Dying Whale," where we see Ishmael again moved to wonder and reverence:

> It was far down in the afternoon; and when all the spearings of the crimson fight were done: and floating in the lovely sunset sea and sky, sun and whale both stilly died together; then, such a sweetness and such plaintiveness, such inwreathing orisons curled up in that rosy air, that it almost seemed as if far over from the deep green convent valleys of the Manilla isles, the Spanish landbreeze, wantonly turned sailor, had gone to sea, freighted with these vesper hymns.

By contrast, the same scene "only soothed [Ahab] to deeper gloom"; somehow it conveyed to him "a wonderousness unknown before," but his ensuing meditation leads him not to consoling reverence, but to a characteristic "lesson": the affirmation of his own "prouder . . . darker faith." Similarly, in what is certainly one of Ahab's most memorable moments, he is moved—in contemplating a sperm whale's head in "The Sphynx"— to a poetic meditation that begins, " 'Speak, thou vast and venerable head.' " (It is the head, of course, that inevitably fascinates Ahab, who sees in it a reflection of himself: " 'Of all divers, thou hast dived the deepest. That head upon which the upper sun now gleams, has moved amid this world's foundations.' ") But what amazes Ahab most is that the head remains silent: " 'O head! thou hast seen enough to split the planets and make an infidel of Abraham, and not one syllable is thine!' " Ahab is momentarily amazed by this capacity for silence, for his own power of speech is his black power of defiance, his pride in the grandeur of his own mind. Thus he ends this meditation characteristically, not in a surrender to some higher power, but in an affirmation of mind: " 'O Nature, and O soul of man! how far beyond all utterance are your linked analogies! not the smallest atom stirs or lives in matter, but has its cunning duplicate in mind."

Ahab is under the spell of mind. And his intellectual pride is most obvious when he defies the lightning: " 'There is some unsuffusing thing beyond thee, thou clear spirit, to whom all thy eternity is but time, all thy creativeness mechanical.' " Like the unrepentant Job, whose story bears an enormous influence on *Moby-Dick*, Ahab would "desire to reason with God." And like the unrepentant Job who spoke "without knowledge, and his words were without wisdom," Ahab fails to see that "we cannot order our speech by reason of darkness" (Job 34:35; 37:19). Forever given to his dark reasoning, Ahab can never really "consider the wondrous works of God" and confess, as Job does, his ignorance of "things too wonderful for me" (Job 42:3). Recalling Melville's remark to Hawthorne—"I have written a wicked book, and feel spotless as the lamb," one might conclude that *Moby-Dick*'s "wickedness" is Ahab's unyielding defiance. But the emphasis of Melville's remark is on his feeling of being cleansed; and corresponding to the confessional tone of this remark, there is an echo of the confessional mode heard throughout the book as Melville (through his selves of Ishmael and Ahab) presses to reveal his deepest religious feelings. Indeed, according to Freedman's historical sketch, the confessional novel is an antecedent to the lyrical novel. But if Melville could not imagine God's direct intervention in his own life—as God intervened from the whirlwind to chastise Job into saving repentance—he could confess his own obsessive power of blackness, personifying it in Ahab, and arrange for it to be consumed in the sea. The peacefulness of "Epilogue"—introduced as it is with its epigraph from Job, "And I only am escaped alone to tell thee"—results from a confessional purgation of Ahab's blackness and corresponds to the peaceful ending of Job, when, having repented "in dust and ashes," Job is silent: then "the Lord also accepted Job."

But the prevailing calm in "Epilogue" is also Melville's emphatic affirmation of his capacity for lyric wonder. *Moby-Dick* is founded in Ishmael's capacity for wonder—not in his "boredom, dread, and despair," as a recent widely credited study claims [Paul Brodtkorb, Jr., *Ishmael's White World: A Phenomenological Reading of Moby-Dick*. New Haven: Yale Univ. Press,

1965]. Through Ishmael's lyric surrenderings to an unfathomable God, *Moby-Dick* centers itself in a peacefulness—forever withheld from Ahab—that corresponds to that place "in the soul of man," wherein "lies one insular Tahiti, full of peace and joy, but encompassed by all the horrors of the half known life. God keep thee! Push not off from that isle, thou canst never return!" Obviously, a precarious peace prevails in what might be called this Tahiti of trust; the struggle within Melville and within the novel is directly reflected by the exclamation, "God keep thee!" And if *Moby-Dick* fully renders the blackness, sharkishness, and death of the natural world, it does so in awe of a Creator of light *and* dark, good *and* evil. Ultimately, the book is the expression of a consciousness that, in the face of madness and evil, can affirm: "amid the tornadoed Atlantic of my being, do I myself still for ever centrally disport in mute calm; and while ponderous planets of unwaning woe revolve round me, deep down and deep inland there I still bathe me in eternal mildness of joy."

Finally, *Moby-Dick* is a celebration of the "ungraspable phantom of *life*" (my emphasis); for, although Ishmael's survival on a life-buoy coffin acknowledges death, it spites death. And as a lyric surrender to the light and dark Creator of life, *Moby-Dick* endures as a wholly American lyrical novel, despite its enormous assimilation of British and Continental influences. It continues to comprehend our Puritan sense of evil as well as our urge for transcendence and innocence, even as it resounds with a more modern sense of ambiguity and emptiness. With all of its learned references, it is a song of wonder in the spirit of Emerson's anti-intellectualism and Whitman's sense that if "I contradict myself," then "Very well . . . I contradict myself." Even more fully than Whitman's song, Melville's contains "multitudes." If Whitman's song celebrates a new American sense of physical and sexual innocence, Melville's has its own sense of erotic innocence to counterpoint its sense of original sin. And far more deeply than Whitman, Melville can sense and accept the darkly disturbing yet primitive innocence of Nature's voraciousness, as imaged, for example, in the "chaste" whiteness of the whale's mouth. Wracked as it certainly is with its sense of evil and voraciousness, *Moby-Dick* remains with *Leaves of Grass* as an American soul song, a lyric launched confidently into the "Measureless oceans of space."

Speech in *Moby-Dick*

Louise K. Barnett

To render the infinitely meaningful and mysterious universe of *Moby-Dick*,
Herman Melville draws upon the languages of drama, exposition, narration,
argument, exhortation, and prophecy, all of which, in the crucible of his
style, are steeped in the same rhetorical intensity and embellishment. This
linguistic richness and exuberance match the wonders of the phenomenological world of the novel and everywhere assert the power of words to
transmute the neutral stuff of reality, the passive beingness of nature, into
subjective visions of meaning and order. As J. L. Austin writes, "Sensa,
that is things, colours, noises, and the rest . . . are dumb, and only previous
experience enables *us* to identify them. If we choose to say that they 'identify
themselves' . . . then it must be admitted that they share the birthright of
all speakers, that of speaking unclearly and untruly." This is the epistemological terrain of the novel: language, the text proposes, can provide a
coherent perspective, a story that may be more or less authorized, but
definitive explanation is beyond its reach—not because of its own inherent
limitations but because the stuff of reality is ultimately intractable to the
sense-making process of language. In Melville's words to Hawthorne, "we
incline to think that God cannot explain His own secrets, and that He would
like a little information upon certain points Himself." Moreover, he spec-
ulates, "perhaps, after all, there is no secret," a void of meaning that no
effort of communication can overcome. In the face of the novel's many
fictive voices and the meditated assault by Captain Ahab, nature remains

From *Studies in American Fiction* 2, no. 2 (Autumn 1983). © 1983 by Northeastern
University.

silent and impenetrable, a condition more frustrating and enraging to Ahab than what he takes to be the wilfully inflicted blows of Moby-Dick. Malignity may be understood and responded to; inscrutability cannot. A man of action and eloquence, Ahab opposes an adversary whose "great genius" is "declared in his pyramidical silence."

Society also presents serious difficulties to the ordering and expressive functions of language, but of a different sort from those in the world of nature; its ground is ethics rather than metaphysics. As hierarchy and institution, society is unfailingly flawed and coercive throughout Melville's fiction, a collection of "civilized hypocrisies and bland deceits"; as community, a locus of shared purpose and feeling, it is fatally ambiguous. The same road to felicity that Ishmael extols in "A Squeeze of the Hand" disintegrates under the feet of Pierre, and Queequeg suspended on the monkey-rope is in equal danger from friend and foe. Seeing his tie to Queequeg here as a symbol of the human condition, which is "a Siamese connexion with a plurality of other mortals," Ishmael offers two further examples of dependence: "If your banker breaks, you snap; if your apothecary by mistake sends you poison in your pills, you die." Whereas the labor of Ishmael and Queequeg is infused with mutual affection, these are instances of impersonal commercial transaction and thus susceptible to the additional hazards of performance divorced from feeling. This state of uncertain dependency is the Melvillian dilemma: isolation warps the spirit, but, through lack of caring, the collective existence can be uncharitable, unjust, and oppressive. Necessary human relationships are menaced by societal rigidity and individual egocentricity but menaced more by the difficulty of distinguishing exploitative forms of authority from those that create genuine community. It is both a "mutual, joint-stock world, in all meridians" and a "wicked world in all meridians," but these partial views, held and harmonized by the noble savage Queequeg, become embodied in Ishmael and Ahab respectively.

Of the two, the sociality and cooperation that Ishmael espouses as the ultimate good of existence, and the cosmic evil that Ahab envisions as the ultimate truth, the atypical nature of most speaking in the novel encourages the negative view that would come to dominate Melville's later fiction, that the world is a place where communication is suspect and perhaps impossible. The self-contained soliloquy, in which speaker and hearer are the same person, is especially suited to Ahab, who admits no one else to his level of being, but it is also used by those in some way committed to a joint-stock world, gregarious Stubb and conformist Starbuck. All of these circumstances portend the linguistic impotence of speakers in Melville's later fiction yet do not diminish the vigor of speech in *Moby-Dick*, most likely because the novel's language was profoundly affected by Melville's recent immersion in Shakespeare, and this influence was expansive and affirmative. Already in *Pierre*, only a year later, the impulse had mostly spent itself, and Melville began to lose control over the kind of long eloquent speech that is consistently effective in *Moby-Dick*. Such rhetorically brilliant set pieces disappear after *Pierre*, as Melville's developing tendency toward verbal skepticism asserts itself in stylistic restraint, but in *Moby-Dick* speech, especially that of Captain Ahab, is charged with a Shakespearian ebullience that challenges the problematic nature of communication.

Considering the unexceptional dialogue of the autobiographical romances preceding *Moby-Dick*, and the increasing attenuation of speech in Melville's later fiction, the many voices that articulate the world of this novel are all the more remarkable. Like the Anacharsis Clootz deputation that was a favorite Melvillian image, the multitude of verbal styles consciously represents the heterogeneous collectively of mankind, a part of the ambitious plenitude that informs all aspects of the novel. This speech is individualized but seldom realistic, pervasively marked as it is by Shakespearian wit and rhetorical extravagance.

Here as elsewhere throughout *Moby-Dick* Melville replicates Ahab's heroic quest for knowledge of the universe by seeking out and testing the limits of literary structures. This exploration of the interface between what can and cannot be said creates a powerful dialectic between confident verbalization and silence, one that Melville establishes in a variety of ways. Because speech is made to bear a weight of philosophic inquiry that would ordinarily be conveyed through narrative alone, it tends to be far more declamatory than conversational. This conjoins with the importance of hierarchical relationships in the novel to produce a number of one-sided speech situations in which speaking is more likely to be some form of exhortation—sermon, order, challenge—or dramatic soliloquy, than normative dialogue. A large block of speech is directed to an audience that lacks full participatory status: the crew of the *Pequod* addressed by Ahab, collectively and individually, the congregation for Father Mapple's sermon, the men in the whaleboats exhorted by their officers during the chase. All of these one-way speech situations, because they are based upon the inequality of speakers, emphasize the omnipresence of a societal order that reduces many would-be speakers to silence. Once the voyage is underway, the only talk exchange on the basis of equality occurs between Stubb and Flask and between Boomer and Bunger on the *Samuel Enderby*. (The latter is a noteworthy exception because, like the relationship of Ishmael and Queequeg, it instances the transcendence of social hierarchy by affection.) Pip is the most extreme example of distortion of speech by societal pressure:

cut off from all community when a society that places little value on his life abandons him, Pip dramatizes the connection between membership within a group and speech by his inability to speak thereafter in a recognizable idiom.

Diverse problems of communication also prevent speech from becoming successful talk exchange. Most of the *Pequod*'s encounters with other ships involve some difficulty ranging from the literal failure to hear words spoken to the divergent purposes of the interacting speech communities. Moreover, a thread of unintelligible utterance is persistently woven into the fabric of discourse. Like the speech of Pip's madness, the arcane language of prophecy that runs through the novel offers glimpses of a tantalizing world of verbal signification beyond the ordinary.

In spite of the seeming abundance of speakers, one voice dominates the speech of *Moby-Dick*. Most of the novel's speech that is not uttered by Ahab is spoken to him or about him or serves to characterize him indirectly. The inconsequentiality of the brief, fragmentary utterances of the sailors in the "Midnight, Forecastle" scene, Stubb's bantering, Flask's materialism, Starbuck's traditional pieties, all emphasize the single-minded commitment to high significance of Ahab's speech.

Although Melville often calls attention to Ahab's physical appearance — the "livid brand" that marks his face, the "barbaric white leg upon which he partly stood," the "crucifixion in his face"—these vivid particulars are supporting rather than primary; above all, Ahab is a powerful voice. Silenced, he would merely be a posture of fortitude or eccentricity or even pathos, whereas through his commanding rhetoric Ahab creates himself as the heroic protagonist as fully as he creates Moby-Dick as the great antagonist he desires, endowing both roles with transcendent significance. (Ahab does not imagine Moby-Dick to embody all evil in the universe, however; the whale is merely the wall "shoved close," the self-aggrandizing symbol that presents itself in Ahab's own life and thus the necessary focus of his quest.)

In a long passage claiming heroic status for Ahab, Melville goes to some length to establish his speech as singular, the product of a direct encounter between exceptional individuality and nature:

> So that there are instances among them of men, who, named
> with Scripture names . . . and in childhood naturally imbibing
> the stately dramatic *thee* and *thou* of the Quaker idiom; still, from
> the audacious, daring, and boundless adventure of their subse-
> quent lives, strangely blend with these unoutgrown peculiarities,

a thousand bold dashes of character, not unworthy a Scandinavian sea-king, or a poetical Pagan Roman. And when these things unite in a man of greatly superior natural force, with a globular brain and a ponderous heart; who has also by the stillness and seclusion of many long night-watches in the remotest waters, and beneath constellations never seen here at the north, been led to think untraditionally and independently; receiving all nature's sweet or savage impressions fresh from her own virgin, voluntary, and confiding breast, and thereby chiefly, but with some help from accidental advantages, to learn a bold and nervous lofty language—that man makes one in a whole nation's census—a mighty pageant creature, formed for noble tragedies.

In spite of the Quaker accoutrements that give his speech an Old Testament grandeur, Ahab is represented as bypassing society in his acquisition of language and learning an idiom that blends the antisocial with the presocial. That Ahab belongs to an interpretive community of one, speaking a "bold and nervous lofty language" ["nervous" in the nineteenth-century sense of "vigorous, powerful, forcible"] beyond the reach of ordinary men, accounts in part for the lack of genuine communications between him and other speakers. It is always Ahab's desire, as Stanley Fish writes of Coriolanus, "to stand alone, without visible or invisible supports, as a natural force. He wants to be independent of society and of the language with which it constitutes itself and its values, seeking instead a language that is the servant of essences he alone can recognize because he alone embodies them." Ahab intends his speech to be an instrument of cosmic confrontation, which explains why he prefers speaking to nature, to the "clear spirit of clear fire" that he addresses in "The Candles" or to the "vast and venerable head" of the whale. And while Ahab frequently laments the refusal of nature to speak, his preference for apostrophizing the inanimate and denying speech rights to other men suggests that he would hardly be comfortable dealing with nature as autonomous speaker.

If Ahab's language cannot succeed in opening a dialogue with nature, neither is it suited to speech with other men, especially the other men to whom it is usually addressed, his unthinking and unknowing crew. Even those extended utterances putatively directed toward some human audience—for instance, the famous pasteboard mask speech—are like soliloquies, dialogues with self divorced from the requirements of the verbal occasion. Since other men exist for Ahab as tools of his will or limited versions of himself, his language is primarily an instrument of self-assertion

and self-validation, not a means of establishing connections with other men
or exploring the world. His utterances are often imperatives, whose aim is
to get "the world to conform to words," as opposed to illocutions, which
get "words to conform to the world." Ahab regards physical reality as a
"magician's glass" which "to each and every man in turn but mirrors back
his own mysterious self." He therefore sees himself everywhere, simulta-
neously imposing his image on the universe and distancing himself from
its separate reality. The special status that Ahab accords Starbuck, Fedallah,
and Pip correlates with his perception of them as partial or exemplary
versions of himself. Starbuck's eye mirrors wife and child, a self that Ahab
has put aside, while Fedallah's eye reflects the mixed nature of the quest,
its promise of suprahuman knowledge and its taint of demonism. Pip,
superficially the opposite of Ahab, gives back to Ahab his sense of his own
cosmic victimization. Resisting more than such limited identification with
other men, Ahab sees himself as a complete being in "grand and lofty
things," the tower, volcano, and mountain fowl of the doubloon.

In keeping with his ideal of godlike power and self-sufficiency, Ahab
projects his most complete self-image onto Moby-Dick, ascribing to it an
intentionality much like the aggressive malevolence that has characterized
his own pursuit of whales: " 'The madness, the frenzy, the boiling blood
and the smoking brow, with which, for a thousand lowerings old Ahab
has furiously, foamingly chased his prey—more a demon than a man!' "
And if the whale is a fatal magnet because he best embodies the inscrutability
of the universe, Ahab sees himself as moved by the same force—"nameless,
inscrutable, unearthly"—and is himself seen by others in similar terms. In
the confrontation with Moby-Dick Ahab seeks knowledge of himself, but
the only language the two have in common is aggression, a condition that
forecloses the possibility of fruitful communication.

As language Ahab's speech is unquestionably magnificent, but as utterance appropriate to a particular occasion it often succeeds only through
its extraverbal qualities. In spite of Ahab's substitution of personal for
societal goals, much of his effectiveness as a speaker is vested in his role as
captain of the ship; he has supreme authority over the speech of his community because social hierarchy gives him the preeminent right to speak
on board the *Pequod* and for the *Pequod* elsewhere—a power that, regardless
of what he says or how he says it, allows him to monopolize speech and
to a large extent control the speech of others.

Dialogue as ritual, in which each utterance is prescribed and the end
result is to confirm a value he already holds, is Ahab's paradigm for verbal
interaction. Unveiling his intention to hunt the white whale, he guides the

mystified crew to verbal responses—seemingly innocuous—that reinforce each step of his unfolding plan and intensify their feeling:

> "And what do ye next, men?"
> "Lower away, and after him!"
> "And what tune is it ye pull to, men?"
> "A dead whale or a stove boat!"
> More and more strangely and fiercely glad and approving, grew the countenance of the old man at every shout; while the mariners began to gaze curiously at each other, as if marvelling how it was that they themselves became so excited at such seemingly purposeless questions.

Here Ahab builds upon his authority by manipulating the speech situation to induce an excitement that the men find baffling but which can readily be accounted for: the unification of the crew in giving Ahab the routine information he requests and the attendant satisfaction at being able to do so, the rhythm of the antiphonal chant, the suspense of a climactic progression, and Ahab's own conspicuous emotion infuse the familiar words with new significance. Given the crew's lack of sophistication, these simple techniques for enhancing speech are enough.

To counter Starbuck's hesitation requires more and different verbal strategies. When Starbuck demurs at Ahab's announced goal, he is first coached to return the desired response—"Art not game for Moby-Dick?"—but when his rejoinder is negative, he is overwhelmed by a torrent of Ahab's words, which make a number of arguments in succession. The "little lower layer" of philosophical explanation with its prologue flattering Starbuck's intellect is followed by a casuistic apology for offending Starbuck, a reference to the crew's wholehearted support of Ahab (implying Starbuck's isolation) and an attempt to devaluate the hunt to routine (" 'tis but to help strike a fin") coupled with a complimentary denomination of Starbuck as "the best lance out of Nantucket." Ahab's speech is a virtuoso performance, a compendium of rhetorical appeals, but as speech act it fails—Starbuck does not obey the command to speak or acknowledge the sense of any of Ahab's arguments, and his later capitulation is brought about by an almost magical emanation of personal force rather than by language: " 'Something shot from my dilated nostrils, he has inhaled it in his lungs. Starbuck now is mine; cannot oppose me now, without rebellion.' "

In all respects Ahab is an awesomely closed system that rejects outright any opposing view or converts it into support. Fedallah's prophecy that hemp alone can kill him can only be—to Ahab's ears—a reference to the gallows, another pledge that he is invulnerable to Moby-Dick. When his mates shrink from serving as cup-bearers to the harpooners, Ahab transforms his own command into an assertion of *their* intentions: " 'I do not order ye; ye will it.' " In speech act terms such a pronouncement is infelicitous because, as Austin puts it, "you can't just make statements about other people's feelings." Ahab, of course, is not describing the mates' feelings but coercively regarding them as projections of his own will.

When a speaker challenges his purpose more openly, Ahab peremptorily withdraws, uninterested in further speech. Verbally assaulted by Gabriel when the *Pequod* meets the *Jereboam*, "Ahab stolidly turned aside." With his own subordinate Stubb, a more definite closure is called for: " 'Begone, or I'll clear the world of thee!' " For speakers of higher status, like Captain Gardiner, Ahab provides something like the expected closure of social discourse, but its mitigating phrases are surrounded and overwhelmed by what Ishmael calls the language of "unconditional and utter rejection":

> "Avast," cried Ahab —"touch not a rope-yarn;" then in a voice that prolongingly moulded every word—"Captain Gardiner, I will not do it. Even now I lose time. Good bye, good bye. God bless ye, man, and may I forgive myself, but I must go. Mr. Starbuck, look at the binnacle watch, and in three minutes from this present instant warn off all strangers; then brace forward again, and let the ship sail as before."

Characteristically, the speech is dominated by imperatives and by the self-reflexiveness of Ahab's verbal style. Blessing by God is wished upon Captain Gardiner and forgiveness of himself *by himself* for Ahab, polarities that encapsulate societal and individual systems of value.

Ahab ordinarily observes the decorum of polite conversation only to the extent that it is essential to acquire intelligence of Moby-Dick; his model of discourse with the world beyond his ship is the unembellished question— "Hast seen the White Whale?"—and an economical answer, preferably the coordinates of Moby-Dick's position. Even when formation is to be had, as it is from Captain Boomer, Ahab's impatience and egotism constantly disrupt the normative process of talk exchange by breaking into the other speaker's narrative with questioning, direction, and interpretation:

> "Presently up breaches from the bottom of the sea a bouncing great whale, with a milky-white head and hump, all crows' feet and wrinkles."

"It was he, it was he!" cried Ahab, suddenly letting out his suspended breath.

"And harpoons sticking in near his starboard fin."

"Aye, aye—they were mine—*my* irons," cried Ahab, exult-ingly—"but on!"

"Give me a chance, then," said the Englishman, good-hu-moredly. "Well, this old great-grandfather, with the white head and hump, runs all afoam into the pod, and goes to snapping furiously at my fast-line."

"Aye, I see!—wanted to part it; free the fast-fish—an old trick—I know him."

Boomer's leisurely and good-humored account of his misfortune describes events without assigning meaning, whereas Ahab's staccato interruptions express the certainty of positive identification and possession: *it was he, they were mine, I know him.* Boomer's story simply gives Ahab raw material for his own compulsive fiction in which attention is almost equally divided between himself and Moby-Dick, between his action which has marked the whale—as the whale has marked him—and his understanding of its behavior. While complaining that nature refuses to speak to him, Ahab is eager to speak for it, to appropriate the whale verbally by asserting his interpretation of it.

Similarly, when he addresses the head of a dead whale Ahab both protests its silence and asserts his own version of its experience: " 'Thou hast seen enough to split the planets and make an infidel of Abraham, and not one syllable is thine!' " His particularization of this experience is in the indicative rather than the subjunctive, a series of incidents introduced by phrases such as "thou hast been" and "thou saw'st."

Ahab's denial of authority to other speakers leads him at times not only to misinterpret or disregard what is said to him but literally to fail to hear it—token of his inability to suffer any dissenting voice. Absorbed in his victory after Starbuck has succumbed to his will, "Ahab did not hear his foreboding invocation; nor yet the low laugh from the hold; nor yet the presaging vibrations of the winds in the cordage; nor yet the hollow flap of the sails against the masts. . . ." As Ahab leaves the ship on the fatal third day of the chase, Pip warns of sharks and calls him back: "But Ahab heard nothing; for his own voice was high-lifted then."

Predicated upon his assumption of superiority over other speakers, Ahab's speech always denies his kinship with other men, both by rejecting outright their statements and requests and by rejecting implicitly the social

igms that their speech invokes. Immediately before the climactic enter with Moby-Dick Ahab faces his single critic and simply talks him
vn, adducing from the mild weather first the serenity of untroubled life
and then the hegemony of fate and death. When Starbuck responds to Ahab's
first speech by recalling Nantucket, Ahab allows himself to enter this vision,
seeing "the far away home" in his eye, but when Starbuck joins the image
of the boy waiting at home to the imperative "let us away!" Ahab chooses
not to look any longer. He begins to speak again himself, shifting his
discourse to fate and death. While Ahab's words enforce his vision of reality
on Starbuck, causing the mate to blanch "to a corpse's hue," the words of
Starbuck and other speakers capture Ahab's acquiescence only momentarily;
he is never persuaded by them because he rejects the institutions that they
invoke and represent. Captain Gardiner, who makes the unvoiced appeal
of a fellow Nantucketer to Ahab, explicitly refers to their mutual fatherhood
and to the Golden Rule, appeals that Starbuck also makes to Ahab. All of
these pleas speak to primitive and essential kinds of relationships, as does
Captain Boomer's attempt to elicit Ahab's agreement about Moby-Dick
on the basis of their common injury. Where Boomer can contemplate the
loss of his arm without rancor, sustained by his friendship with Bunger,
Ahab's grandiose concept of self cannot assimilate either the violation of
bodily integrity or its resulting dependency.

For all of its testing of literary boundaries and all of Melville's dark
allusions to its lack of orthodoxy, *Moby-Dick* does not finally deviate from
the conventional ideology of nineteenth-century fiction: the individualistic
hero is destroyed and social and even cosmic equilibrium restored at novel's
end. Applying to the language of *Moby-Dick* David L. Minter's useful idea
of the interpreted design, where a "man of design or action" is juxtaposed
to a "man of interpretation," the obsessed and inflexible speech of Ahab,
the character with a goal to achieve, exists within the controlling idiom of
Ishmael, his narrator. It is not so much Ahab's inevitable defeat that gives
the novel its ultimate meaning but the enclosure of Ahab's story and his
egocentric rhetoric within Ishmael's more inclusive vision and language.
For society's economic criteria of value Ahab substitutes his personal goals,
yet the society of the *Pequod* reconstituted in his own image is no less
exploitative, and the view of mankind upon which it is predicated is equally
dehumanized.

Ishmael, on the other hand, begins as someone who goes to sea because
of impulses that make him unfit for society, but he is purged of his antisocial
feelings by his commitment first to Queequeg and then, in "A Squeeze of
the Hand," to humanity in general. Intellectually saved by repudiating the

narrowed perspective of Ahab's quest, and physically saved by the caring of others (the search of the *Rachel* for her missing children), he is returned to a society whose common totems—"the wife, the heart, the bed, the table, the saddle, the fire-side, the country"—he now willingly embraces. Ishmael tells Ahab's tale, but his own encompassing vision rebukes Ahab's restricted view as his survival rebukes Ahab's quest. Where Ahab errs, it seems clear, is in sacrificing others to his egocentric interpretation of reality. Turning his back on the values of community, he imposes the fictions of the autonomous self on his hapless crew.

Disvaluing speech with other men in his desire to have a dialogue with speechless nature, Ahab inevitably experiences the tragedy of isolation that lack of communication and lack of community entail. Where Ahab's sense of importance creates a language of self-validation that functions only in a circular fashion, Ishmael is, in Edgar A. Dryden's words, a "verbal wanderer," able to entertain and articulate numerous perspectives and correspondingly free from hierarchical prejudice. Where Ahab constantly interposes hierarchy between himself and other speakers, creating barriers to free communication, Ishmael overcomes societal barriers to achieve a dialogue with Queequeg.

Yet Ahab is not destroyed because his assumed posture does not finally correspond to the facts. The Ahabean reading of the universe is a self-fulfilling prophecy, enforceable because nature, as Melville wrote in *Pierre*, "is not so much her own ever-sweet interpreter, as the mere supplier of that cunning alphabet, whereby selecting and combining as he pleases, each man reads his own peculiar mind and mood." Whatever physical reality is remains elusive, and the catastrophic meeting with Moby-Dick is exactly the kind of conclusion that Ahab's belief in wilful malignity inscribes upon the universe, a confirmation that man cannot strike through the mask to absolute knowledge. Ishmael's description of this end—"retribution, swift vengeance, eternal malice were in his [Moby-Dick's] whole aspect"—valorizes Ahab's perspective. The necessary criticism of Ahab's language is not its failure to conform to "reality" but its basic violation of what H. Paul Grice has called the Cooperative Principle, the basic assumption of all talk exchange. As a speaker Ahab abrogates this linguistic social contract through his solipsistic indifference to the rights of other men, other speakers.

In keeping with his function as observer rather than hero, comic rather than tragic protagonist, Ishmael is both more pragmatic and more speculative than Ahab; the metaphysical uncertainties that torment Ahab are only one part of his vision of the universe. As the chapter on the whiteness of the whale especially suggests, Ishmael's language accordingly reflects a holistic desire to embrace rather than cut off possibility. Nevertheless, the tempting equation of Ishmael's attitude to Melville's needs to be resisted, for Melville's praxis proposes an integration of comic and tragic worlds in *Moby-Dick,* not a choice between them.

The Metaphysics of Beauty and Terror in *Moby-Dick*

Frank G. Novak, Jr.

As the *Pequod* enters the cruising grounds where she will eventually encounter Moby-Dick, a typhoon suddenly disrupts the beauty and calm of "these resplendent Japanese seas." The typhoon, Ishmael says, "will sometimes burst from out that cloudless sky, like an exploding bomb upon a dazed and sleepy town." Yet this phenomenon of unexpected terror suddenly erupting amidst peaceful beauty is not unusual; indeed, as Ishmael observes, it commonly occurs in nature: "Warmest climes but nurse the cruellest fangs: the tiger of Bengal crouches in the spiced groves of ceaseless verdure. Skies the most effulgent but basket the deadliest thunders: gorgeous Cuba knows tornadoes that never swept tame northern lands."

This passage exemplifies a motif, a symbolic and thematic pattern, which pervades *Moby-Dick*. This recurrent motif consists of a binary opposition between beauty and terror. In the basic form of the motif, the appearance of beauty deceptively conceals the terror which inevitably lurks beneath the surface. The binary opposition of beauty and terror comprises the basic symbolic structure and thematic intent of many descriptive passages and, in a broader sense, sustains a dialectical tension which informs the entire novel. The beauty-terror dichotomy appears in a variety of combinations; it is often a contrast between physical appearances such as cats and tigers, days and nights, the ocean's surfaces and depths, male and female. These physical opposites frequently possess a metaphysical significance by symbolizing the difference between such concepts as thought and emotion,

From *Studies in the Novel* 15, no. 4 (Winter 1983). © 1983 by North Texas State University. Originally entitled " 'Warmest Climes but Nurse the Cruellest Fangs': The Metaphysics of Beauty and Terror in *Moby-Dick*."

inner realities and outward appearances, truth and illusion. The novel is, of course, replete with dual oppositions—good-evil, order-chaos, Christian-pagan, and so forth. Such symbolic and thematic tensions can be generally stated in terms of the opposition between beauty and terror; in other words, many of the forces or qualities which exist in binary opposition can be subsumed under the beauty-terror paradigm. Underlying many individual passages describing natural scenes as well as the overall symbolic structure, the beauty-terror opposition is the pervasive, the most consistently developed binary contrast in the novel. The contrast developed by this motif produces an effect, a tension which animates many of the novel's descriptive and symbolic passages: the more beautiful the scene or image, the more ominous and malevolent is the terror associated with it.

As a pervasive symbolic structure, the beauty-terror opposition is a fundamental form of what Charles Feidelson calls the novel's "primal patterns of conflict." Starbuck's tendency to discern "inward presentiments" in "outward portents" generally describes the way the universe is perceived in the book. This view also suggests a method of interpreting the images of binary opposition. Describing the dangers of waging war against the whale, Ishmael speaks of "the interlinked terrors and wonders of God." This association of terror with wonder, Starbuck's "inward presentiment" ironically signified by the "outward portent," resonates powerfully throughout the novel. In "A Bower in the Arsacides," for example, the pattern is developed in terms of the intimate juxtaposition of life and death; as the vines covered the skeleton of the whale, "Life folded Death; Death trellised Life; the grim god wived with youthful Life, and begat him curly-headed glories." Ishmael's description of the whale line contains the same sort of contrast: "the graceful repose of the line, as it silently serpentines about the oarsmen before being brought into actual play . . . carries more of true terror than any other aspect of this dangerous affair." Whalemen, he contends, routinely encounter "virgin wonders and terrors." And the fact that "the incorruption of this most fragrant ambergris should be found in the heart of such decay" is typical of the many connected opposites one encounters at sea. These contrasts are at the heart of a basic symbolic and thematic pattern: the dual motif, the binary opposition of beauty and terror. Not incidentally do the passages which describe this startling but natural association of beauty and terror rank among the most poetic and powerful in the novel, containing rich, highly suggestive imagery and a sense of dramatic tension evoked by the contrast. The tension produced by the contrast charges these passages with a high level of poetic energy.

The beauty-terror antithesis which appears so frequently in *Moby-Dick* is adumbrated in Melville's review "Hawthorne and His Mosses." Here Melville asserts that the mind which possesses greatness and genius not only perceives the delightful, beautiful surfaces of life but also grapples with the terrors of existence which lie beneath; a recognition of life's beauty and joy must be accompanied by an awareness of what he calls the "power of blackness." The writer of genius possesses a highly developed sense of "humor and love," yet these sunny qualities must be complemented by "a great, deep intellect, which drops down into the universe like a plummet." Melville describes what he sees as the characteristic juxtaposition of beauty and terror, happiness and despair, joy and suffering manifest in Hawthorne's stories. In terms of both image and idea, several passages in the review presage what becomes a recurrent pattern in *Moby-Dick*: Melville notes the familiar "Indian-summer sunlight on the hither side of Hawthorne's soul," yet he emphasizes the other side which "is shrouded in a blackness." One should not be deceived by superficial appearances in Hawthorne, he says, for though one "may be witched by his sunlight . . . there is the blackness of darkness beyond." This basic dichotomy of a dark, terrifying underside beneath the deceptive surface of beauty and mildness appears again and again in *Moby-Dick*, especially in descriptions of natural phenomena. It is part and parcel of the basic imagistic and symbolic pattern of the novel. Melville recognized this polarity in Hawthorne, a symbolic pattern reflecting a tragic sense of life, and incorporated a similar binary structure into *Moby-Dick*.

There are four basic patterns by which the binary opposition of beauty and terror is developed in various descriptive passages. The first pattern contrasts the superficial loveliness and calmness of a mild day at sea with the destructive forces concealed beneath the surface of the ocean. Passages of this pattern simply indicate or describe a startling contrast and depict what Ishmael apparently accepts as a fact of nature. In "The Gilder," for example, Ishmael describes floating upon the calm ocean in pleasant weather: "The soft waves themselves, that like hearth-stone cats they purr against the gunwale; there are the times of dreamy quietude, when beholding the tranquil beauty and brilliancy of the ocean's skin, one forgets the tiger heart that pants beneath it; and would not willingly remember, that this velvet paw but conceals a remorseless fang." "The Symphony" presents a similar scene which is developed in terms of male-female opposition: "Hither, and thither, on high, glided the snow-white wings of small, unspeckled birds; these were the gentle thoughts of the feminine air; but to and fro in the deeps, far down in the bottomless blue, rushed mighty leviathans, sword-fish, and sharks; and these were the strong, troubled, murderous thinkings of the masculine sea." This polarity of surface beauty and submerged terror, a juxtaposition of gentle creatures with savage ones, is an inherent quality of nature. In the above passage, the sexual differentiation merely hints at the profound differences hidden within—as Ishmael continues: "But though thus contrasting within, the contrast was only in shades and shadows without; those two seemed one; it was only the sex, as it were, that distinguished them." In this pattern, surface beauty belies the terror and horror which exist beneath. While fast to the aged whale, "the three boats lay there on that gently rolling sea, gazing down into its eternal blue noon," yet "beneath all that silence and placidity, the utmost monster of the seas was writhing and wrenching in agony!" These passages, presenting the binary motif in its most literal form, contain a straightforward message: one should beware of the terrors which are deceptively interlinked with the beauties of the sea. The sea's beautiful surface but masks bloodthirsty sharks lurking in the depths; there is a "tiger heart" beneath a velvet exterior.

Another manifestation of the binary opposition juxtaposes a tangible phenomenon with its intangible opposite. A physical scene of natural beauty evokes an inward, metaphysical terror of the mind. In a variation of the motif in which a beautiful scene is accompanied by a reminder that terror constantly lurks nearby, here a recognition of physical beauty paradoxically leads to a confrontation with the terror latent within each person. In a passage lush with sensuous imagery, Ishmael describes the beautiful days and nights encountered as the *Pequod* enters tropical waters: "The warmly cool, clear, ringing, perfumed, overflowing, redundant days, were as crystal goblets of Persian sherbet, heaped up—flaked up, with rose-water snow. The starred and stately nights seemed haughty dames in jewelled velvets. . . . For sleeping man, 'twas hard to choose between such winsome days and such seducing nights." But there is a hint of foreboding and terror even here. Far from producing a soporific or calming effect, such beauties work upon the soul engendering a disturbed brooding, a restless fear: "But all the witcheries of that unwaning weather did not merely lend new spells and potencies to the outward world. Inward they turned upon the soul, especially when the still mild hours of eve came on; then, memory shot her crystals as the clear ice most forms of noiseless twilights. And all these subtle agencies, more and more they wrought on Ahab's texture." While the passages cited earlier describe a beautiful facet of nature inevitably accompanied by a malign aspect, the lovely days and nights described in this passage have their terrible complement in the mind. As the *Pequod* leaves "ice and icebergs all astern" and enters tropical climes, the ship encounters another type of glacial threat: the nameless terrors whose frozen crystals are etched on the mind. In this instance, physical beauty poetically and paradoxically suggests its metaphysical opposite. In context, of course, the beauties of nature trigger dark thoughts particularly in the mind of Ahab; yet the passage generally implies that Ishmael, and possibly other members of the crew as well, also know the chilling terrors of memory. Ishmael does not explain exactly how or why this connection takes place. Perhaps one's sins and imperfections become more sharply defined when contrasted with the serene perfection of natural beauty; perhaps these blissful tropical scenes are undermined by the terrors of death, addressed elsewhere by Ahab as the "dark Hindoo half of nature, who of drowned bones hast builded thy separate throne somewhere in the heart of these unverdured seas." In any event, scenes of beauty, by means of "witcheries," can turn inward upon the soul where terror and evil lurk.

In a third pattern of binary opposition, a phenomenon of nature can assume either a beautiful or terrifying appearance depending upon one's perspective. The example here is Ishmael's metaphorical description of Pip's transformation occurring as a result of his hours at sea as a castaway. While drifting for hours on the ocean, the innocent, happy cabin boy confronts the terrifying realities of existence, goes insane—according to conventional notions of insanity—and becomes the intimate of the even madder Ahab. As a result of viewing the "hoarded heaps" of wisdom and the "joyous, heartless, ever-juvenile eternities," the simple servant boy acquires forbidden knowledge and becomes the king's philosopher. Melville explains this metamorphosis by comparing Pip to a beautiful diamond:

> So, though in the clear air of day, suspended against a blue-veined neck, the pure-watered diamond drop will healthful glow; yet, when the cunning jeweller would show you the diamond in its most impressive lustre, he lays it against a gloomy ground, and then lights it up, not by the sun, but by some unnatural gases. Then come out those fiery effulgences, infernally superb; then the evil-blazing diamond, once the divinest symbol of the crystal skies, looks like some crown-jewel stolen from the King of Hell.

Here a natural object ostensibly displays a benign, salubrious beauty from one point of view but when viewed in a different light reveals an "evil-blazing" terror, emanating from sinister, satanic forces. Without undergoing structural change, the diamond with a "healthful glow" becomes the "crown-jewel" of the "King of Hell." It is at once the symbol of both good

ıty and terror: its meaning varies with the viewer's perspective.
ıistic pattern, a tangible object—Pip, the diamond, whiteness,
le—may signify innocence or evil, beauty or terror.

... the final variation of the binary motif as it appears in descriptive passages, the inevitable juxtaposition of terror and beauty in the natural world has its metaphysical counterpart. In other words, terror accompanies beauty in abstract, metaphysical realms just as in the physical world. In "Brit" Ishmael describes the polarity which typically exists in nature: "Consider the subtleness of the sea; how its most dreaded creatures glide under water, unapparent for the most part, and treacherously hidden beneath the loveliest tints of azure. Consider also the devilish brilliance and beauty of many of its most remorseless tribes, as the dainty embellished shape of many species of sharks." This link between terror and beauty in the natural world suggests an analogy with the realms of the soul where a similar connection, another "subtleness," exists: "do you not find a strange analogy to something in yourself? For as this appalling ocean surrounds the verdant land, so in the soul of man there lies one insular Tahiti, full of peace and joy, but encompassed by all the horrors of the half known life." In the metaphysical universe, however, the general pattern is reversed: beauty, the "insular Tahiti," lies at the heart of or concealed beneath terror—the "horrors of the half known life." A similar idea and symbolic pattern are presented in "The Grand Armada" where Ishmael observes the contrast between the "consternations and affrights" of the whales at the perimeter of the great school and the peaceful serenity of those at the center. This external, physical juxtaposition has its inward, philosophical corollary: "amid the tornadoed Atlantic of my being, do I myself still forever centrally disport in mute calm; and while ponderous planets of unwaning woe revolve round me, deep down and deep inland there I still bathe me in eternal mildness of joy." There is a serene beauty residing beneath the savage, terrifying appearance of Queequeg. Possessing a "Sublime" serenity, a "calm self-collectedness of simplicity," Queequeg nourishes a philosophical repose similar to that "insular Tahiti" which Ishmael elsewhere describes. Though wild and terrifying in appearance, Queequeg is a "soothing savage" who "redeems" the "wolfish world" from Ishmael's "splintered heart and maddened hand." In the natural world, the terror and malevolence which insidiously lurk beneath the surface of beauty, according to Melville's general pattern, are ultimately triumphant or, at least, unopposed. However, as the above examples indicate, in the metaphysical realm an inward sense of peace, joy, and beauty—if carefully nourished—can resist whatever terrors might beset the individual. An "insular Tahiti" of serenity and beauty can be a safe haven from the terrors of "tornadoed Atlantics" and "ponderous planets of unwaning woe"—what Ishmael elsewhere calls "the universal thump" which everyone will receive "either in a physical or metaphysical point of view."

Melville not only uses the binary opposition motif in individual descriptive or philosophical passages; he also develops the same themes and symbolic patterns on a more comprehensive scale. The association of beauty with terror, of course, often appears in descriptions of the white whale himself. One effect of the cetological chapters is to impart a sense both of the whale's magnificent beauty and his terrible, destructive power. When first sighted, Moby-Dick, unprovoked, is a creature of serene beauty, but his beauty is accompanied by an awesome capacity for violence and terror:

> A gentle joyousness—a mighty mildness of repose in swiftness, invested the gliding whale. Not the white bull Jupiter swimming away with ravished Europa clinging to his graceful horns . . . did surpass the glorified White Whale as he so divinely swam. . . . No wonder there had been some among the hunters who namelessly transported and allured by all that serenity, had ventured to assail it; but had fatally found that quietude but the vesture of tornadoes. . . . And thus, through the serene tranquillities of the tropical sea, among waves whose hand-clappings were suspended by exceeding rapture, Moby Dick moved on, still withholding from sight the full terrors of his submerged trunk, entirely hiding the wrenched hideousness of his jaw.

Or when the whale breaches, the scene is one of stunning color and beauty:

> as in his immeasurable bravadoes the White Whale tossed himself salmon-like to Heaven. So suddenly seen in the blue plain of the sea, and relieved against the still bluer margin of the sky, the spray that he raised, for the moment, intolerably glittered and glared like a glacier; and stood there gradually fading and fading away from its first sparkling intensity, to the dim mistiness of an advancing shower in a vale.

Yet when attacked, Moby-Dick becomes a creature of malevolent fury who ruthlessly destroys his pursuers; in his next appearance, the whale strikes a "quick terror" in the pursuing crew by "rushing among the boats with open jaws, and a lashing tail," offering "appalling battle on every side . . . intent on annihilating each separate plank of which those boats were made." The whale, therefore, embodies the principle that, in nature, beauty is closely accompanied by terror; like the diamond symbolizing Pip, the salient attribute of the whale depends on one's perspective. Recounting "The Town-Ho's Story," Ishmael describes "the appalling beauty of the vast milky mass, that lit up by a horizontal spangling sun, shifted and glistened like a living opal in the blue morning sea." The phrase "appalling beauty" is used again to describe the whale's tail "where infantileness of ease undulates through a Titanism of power." Moby-Dick, as it were, conspires with nature to vanquish his frustrated pursuers in scenes which are at once both beautiful and terrifying: "amid the chips of chewed boats, and sinking limbs of torn comrades, they swam out of the white curds of the whale's direful wrath into the serene, exasperating sunlight, that smiled on, as if at a birth or a bridal."

This paradoxical, dual symbolism of Moby-Dick is explored in "The Whiteness of the Whale." Here Ishmael grants the familiar significance of the color which suggests beauty, goodness, and purity; but he argues that under close scrutiny white ultimately connotes a paralyzing terror of the unknown. "Though in many natural objects," he says, "whiteness refiningly enhances beauty . . . there yet lurks an elusive something in the innermost idea of this hue, which strikes more of panic to the soul than that redness which affrights in blood." This paradox, he maintains, is the essential quality of whiteness: "it is at once the most meaning symbol of spiritual things, nay, the very veil of the Christian's Deity; and yet should be as it is, the intensifying agent in things the most appalling to mankind." Conforming to the general pattern of the binary motif, the discussion of whiteness contrasts outward beauty with inward terror. The dual symbolism of whiteness is grounded in the basic assumption that unseen terrors lurk beneath the surface of beauty: "Though in many of its aspects this visible world seems formed in love, the invisible spheres were formed in fright." As the "visible absence of color," whiteness represents the unseen, unknown world beneath or beyond the visible world of tangible, physical reality—which it also symbolizes by being "the concrete of all colors." Ultimately, therefore, white evokes the terror of nothingness; as Melville says: "it shadows forth the heartless voids and immensities of the universe, and thus stabs us from behind with the thought of annihilation." The ultimate significance of whiteness is essentially identical to the tragic emptiness, the "blackness of darkness," Melville discerned in Hawthorne. Like the typhoon suddenly bursting from cloudless skies, the terror of whiteness strikes without warning. As the essence of light, whiteness exemplifies the deceptive quality of all physical appearances, beautiful though they may be: "all deified Nature absolutely paints like the harlot, whose allurements cover nothing but the charnel-house within." While superficially benign, whiteness, then, deceptively evokes terrifying uncertainties—just as the azure surface of the sea barely conceals the bloodthirsty terrors lurking beneath, just as the beautiful days and nights of tropical climes engender frozen thoughts of dark terror in the mind, just as the white whale himself is at once a creature of intense beauty and annihilating terror. As the primary symbol of this dichotomy, Moby Dick embodies the inevitable juxtaposition of beauty with terror, in the physical world as well as in the metaphysical realm.

A recognition of the beauty-terror dualism is also fundamental to an understanding of Ahab, who dramatically reveals the tensions between the two poles. As part of the general pattern in which terror insidiously lurks beneath the surface of beauty, Ahab's maniacal quest taints the idyllic beauty of the ocean scenes which the *Pequod* and her crew encounter. The terror of Ahab's dark thoughts and suicidal quest opposes the benign beauties of the natural world. Ahab acknowledges the beauty of the sunset, for example, but he is incapable of enjoying its loveliness: "This lovely light, it lights not me; all loveliness is anguish to me, since I can ne'er enjoy. Gifted with the high perception, I lack the low, enjoying power; damned, most subtly and most malignantly! damned in the midst of Paradise!" Throughout the novel Ahab demonstrates an awareness of the binary opposition. According to his dualistic view, there is an "inscrutable malice" behind the "pasteboard masks" of "visible objects." While he temporarily responds to the beauty of the mild day described in "The Symphony," the "cankerous thing in his soul" abruptly dispels his pleasant reverie and fond thoughts of home. The inevitable terrors of his mad quest lurk behind the superficial beauties of that winsome day, which momentarily affects Ahab and causes him to drop a tear into the sea; seeing this, Ishmael observes that the "sweet childhood of air and sky" are "oblivious" to "old Ahab's close-coiled woe." Although the beauties of nature exert at least a temporary effect on Ahab, opening in him "secret golden treasures, yet did his breath upon them prove but tarnishing." While Ahab's terrible thoughts and ambition despoil the beauties of the natural world, he sees, paradoxically, a sort of beauty in the terrors he must confront. He believes that "all heart-woes" have "a mystic significance" and, occasionally, "an archangelic grandeur"; "mortal miseries," he thinks, have their origins in the "sourceless primogenitures of the gods." Yet this "divine" beauty which evolves from terror leads inescapably to a species of ultimate terror which the gods themselves cannot overcome: "so that, in the face of all the glad, hay-making suns, and soft-cymballing, round harvest-moons, we must needs give into this: that the gods themselves are not for ever glad." Unlike Queequeg and Ishmael, who are apparently able to maintain a serene "insular Tahiti" within themselves, Ahab's soul nourishes a dark madness, "a cunning and most feline thing." Ishmael compares this "larger, darker, deeper part" lurking in Ahab to the "vast Roman halls of Thermes" underground beneath the apparently "grand and wonderful" Hotel de Cluny. In these subterranean halls, "far beneath the fantastic towers of man's upper earth . . . his whole awful essence sits in bearded state; an antique buried beneath antiquities, and throned on torsoes!" For Ahab beauty exists only externally, terror is the inner reality: "So far gone am I in the dark side of earth, that its other side, the theoretic bright one, seems but uncertain twilight to me."

Melville's pervasive use of the beauty-terror motif suggests at least two general observations. First of all, the novel argues that entities have reality or can be defined only by contrast with their opposites. As Ishmael observes: "truly to enjoy bodily warmth, some small part of you must be cold, for there is no quality in this world that is not what it is merely by contrast. Nothing exists in itself." In fact, contrasting opposites comprise the essential fabric of existence. As much as one might wish happiness to endure, "the mingled, mingling threads of life are woven by warp and woof; calms crossed by storms, a storm for every calm. There is no steady unretracing progress in this life; we do not advance through fixed gradations, and at the last one pause." Ishmael consistently establishes the pattern in which scenes that are calm and "monotonously mild" inevitably presage "some riotous and desperate scene." The "alluring" but dangerous "spirit-spout" is first descried on a "serene and moonlight night"; this ghostly phenomenon "derived a wondrous potency from the contrasting serenity of the weather, in which, beneath all its blue blandness, some thought there lurked a devlish charm." The ominous, terrifying squid is sighted on a "transparent blue morning . . . when the long burnished sun-glade on the waters seemed a golden finger laid across them." Not surprisingly, each of the three days of the chase is one of supreme beauty—contrasting with the destructive terror of the white whale. The fundamental component of life itself, Ishmael argues, consists of contrasting forces set in binary opposition, each giving reality, identity, or significance to its counterpart. Beauty or terror, therefore, can be defined only in terms of its opposite. This antithesis occasionally evolves into a synthesis: just as "there is a wisdom that is woe," there is also a beauty which is terror. The white whale, of course, is the embodiment of this synthesis.

Second, the juxtaposition of beauty and terror as an inherent quality of nature holds significance in terms of Emersonian symbolism. Ahab clearly states the link which is assumed throughout the novel: "O Nature, and O soul of Man! how far beyond all utterance are your linked analogies! not the smallest atom stirs or lives in matter, but has its cunning duplicate in mind." One is reminded of Emerson's basic premise: "Every natural fact is a symbol of some spiritual fact." According to Ishmael, the juxtaposition of beauty and terror in the natural world has its counterpart in the metaphysical realm. Beauty, goodness, and joy, on one side, are counterbalanced by terror, evil, and suffering on the other—in the world empirically perceived or in Emerson's "apocalypse of the mind." Starbuck, ever the pious optimist, relishes the beauty of the day described in "The Gilder," yet he knows that beneath the dazzlingly beautiful surface lie "teeth-tiered sharks" and "kidnapping cannibal ways." The reality, the supremacy of these terrors can be denied only by letting "faith oust fact" and "fancy oust memory." Depending on one's philosophical or theological perspective, however, the scales may be weighted toward either pole. As far as Ahab is concerned, "every revelation partook more of significant darkness than of explanatory light." Yet Father Mapple asserts that "on the starboard hand of every woe, there is a sure delight; and higher the top of that delight, than the bottom of the woe is deep." Whatever the case, the novel repeatedly demonstrates that for every softly purring "hearth-stone cat" there is a terrifying "painting tiger"—and that each creature conceals a "remorseless fang" within a "velvet claw."

A simple yet powerful symbolic structure, the binary opposition, structuralist theorists argue, serves "as a fundamental operation of the human mind basic to the production of meaning." Bruno Bettelheim's interpretation of Freudian analysis underscores the significance of the binary opposition and suggests why it is such a pervasive structure in *Moby-Dick*. According to Bettelheim, the Eros-Thanatos antithesis is at the heart of Freud's thought and theory. These two forces "struggle for dominance in shaping our lives," and this struggle creates a tension which gives life intensity and meaning. Because a life emphasizing either extreme will be warped and empty, there must be constant mediation between the happy and the tragic, between optimism and pessimism. Poets, Bettelheim observes, have been particularly sensitive to the necessity of this conflict which both endows life with a tragic dimension and accounts for man's highest, most satisfying achievements. Similarly, in *Moby-Dick* the threat of inevitable terror heightens the sense of beauty. This tension not only delineates and intensifies both beauty and terror but, as seen above, can also merge one with the other. Out of the continuous dialectic between the two, borrowing a line from Yeats, "a terrible beauty is born." Yet the novel does not advance a synthesis in which one emerges triumphant. In nature and in the mind, beauty and terror exist, paradoxically, only in tandem. To understand fully the distinctions between the two and, consequently, the ultimate nature of each comprises a vexing riddle—which, like the meaning of Queequeq's tattoos, remains a "devilish tantalization of the gods."

Ahab's Name:
A Reading of "The Symphony"

P. Adams Sitney

Is Ahab, Ahab?

In "The Symphony," chapter 132 of *Moby-Dick*, the captain's dialogue with his first mate, Starbuck, drifts into a soliloquy in which he questions his control over his acts:

> What is it, what nameless, inscrutable, unearthly thing is it; what cozening, hidden lord and master, and cruel remorseless emperor commands me; that against all natural lovings and longings, I so keep pushing, and crowding and jamming myself on all the time; recklessly making me ready to do what in my own proper, natural heart, I durst not so much as dare? Is Ahab, Ahab? Is it I, God or who, that lifts this arm? But if the great sun move not of himself; but is as an errand-boy in heaven; nor one single star can revolve, but by some invisible power; how can this one small heart beat; this one small brain think thoughts; unless God does that beating, does that thinking, does that living, and not I.

In this context the tiny sentence "Is Ahab, Ahab?" appears innocent enough. The force of fate makes the captain doubt his identity. For years I read this question ignoring the comma, supporting myself with the commonplace of editors that Melville was an ungrammatical punctuator, as if

---

the sentence were the interrogative form of the tautology: Ahab is Ahab. But what might the question "Is Ahab Ahab?" or "Is X X?" when X stands for a proper noun, mean? In the form of a question doubt is raised about the *language* of the tautology. It asks if there is not something wrong with the naming of X that represents X as ontologically unstable. Then again, it could be a question about two different meanings of the proper noun. Does the first X correspond fully to the stable meaning of X represented by the second instance of the name? All three readings of the question are relevant to our interpretation of *Moby-Dick* as a whole: they correspond to ontological, epistemological, and typological investigations.

I would like to consider the alternatives posed by the problematic comma. If we read the second naming of Ahab as vocative, two interpretations of the sentence are possible. Either "Is Ahab?" questions his existence, or the sentence is incomplete, requiring reference to the previous one. In that case it asks if "Ahab" is the answer to the previous question; is "Ahab" the "nameless . . . thing" that "commands me." In fact, the first English edition of *The Whale*, printed months earlier than the American, explicitly determines this reading. "Is it Ahab, Ahab?" in the English text makes very good sense, for it fits all three opening sentences in this speech into a single form: "What is it? Is it Ahab? Is it I, God, or who?"

We cannot conclude whether this is one of the many editorial intrusions to be found in *The Whale* or a genuine alternative from Melville's hand. Let's consider the consequences of accepting it as the superior reading. The ontological question posed by both "Is Ahab Ahab?" and "Is Ahab?" disappears. Nevertheless, the repetition of the name in the vocative continues to underscore the potential ambiguity of the name, which has both epistemological and typological consequences. It is this doubling of the *name*, consistent in both texts, which I take to be crucial; for it points up the relationship of the name to the dilemmas of identity and responsibility. Therefore, even though I prefer the richer ambiguities of the American version, what follows will not depend upon the choice of texts.

My conviction that "Is Ahab, Ahab?" should be read as the questioning of a tautology rests on the echoing passage two chapters later in "The Chase—Second Day" when the captain refers back to his earlier encounter with the first mate:

> Starbuck, of late I've felt strangely moved to thee; ever since that hour we both saw—thou know'st what, in one another's eyes. But in this matter of the whale, be thy face to me as the palm of this hand—a lipless, unfeatured blank. Ahab is for ever

> Ahab, man. This whole act's immutably decreed. 'Twas re-
> hearsed by thee and me a billion years before this ocean rolled.
> Fool! I am the Fates' lieutenant; I act under orders.

"Ahab is for ever Ahab, man" reasserts the ontological question of the earlier chapter in the rhetoric of bravado, taking the tautology out of the realm of time which had oppressed the captain, who feared that Moby-Dick would be taken by a rival whaler or that he would not live to do the job. Now that he is in the midst of the "fiery hunt," he speaks as though he were reconciled to his relationship to Fate. But readers soon discover that he is haunted during this speech by hints of the fulfillment of Fedallah's prophecy of his death.

The paired lines "Is Ahab, Ahab?" and "Ahab is for ever Ahab" do not dispell the ambiguities we found in the name, Ahab. The later speech proclaims that Ahab is an ontological entity, that his name is appropriate, and that he conforms to the model of the ancient, Biblical Ahab.

The tone of these speeches is familiar enough. Melville wrote fresh from a reading of Shakespeare. The use of the name, instead of "I," in the mouth of the hero recalls a number of precedents in the plays.

> O Lear, Lear, Lear!
> Beat at this gate, that let thy folly in
> And thy dear judgment out!
> (King Lear, I, iv)

> Was't Hamlet wronged Laertes? Never Hamlet.
> If Hamlet from himself be ta'en away,
> And when he's not himself does wrong Laertes,
> Then Hamlet does it not, Hamlet denies it.
> Who does it then? His madness. If it'd be so,
> Hamlet is of the faction that is wronged,
> His madness is poor Hamlet's enemy.
> (Hamlet, V, ii)

Shakespeare uses this substitution of the third for the first person, of the name for I, here and in parallel speeches by Othello, Brutus, and Timon, to emphasize the machinations of fate or to dramatize the dislocation of selfhood in madness. Its illusion of objectivity indicates that the speaker has submitted to the language and the judgment of the world by renouncing his power to speak for himself. To make such a renunciation is to invoke the discourse of the victim.

Melville became excessively fond of this mode of self-address. It is a mark of Ahab's grandiosity. Interpreting the Ecuadorian doubloon he nailed to the mast as a reward for the first sighting of Moby-Dick, he repeats his name four times: "The firm tower, that is Ahab; the volcano, that is Ahab; the courageous, undaunted, and victorious fowl, that, too, is Ahab; all are Ahab; and this round gold is but the image of the rounder globe, which, like a magician's glass, to each and every man in turn but mirrors back its own mysterious self." As much echo as mirror, the coin reflects his name again and again.

In *Moby-Dick* calling oneself by name is not Ahab's exclusive privilege. Stubb does it with comic effect when he finds himself unfairly treated by the captain. The narrator calls himself by his pseudonym three times in "A Bower in the Arsacides," as if, taking the side of his readers, he felt the need to demand evidence of his authority for the whalelore he was about to expound. These whimsical versions of the discourse of victimage are not of the same order of frequency or dramatic intensity as Ahab's use of his own name. He embraces and sublimates his victimage, naming himself as if being called Ahab were an honor and a responsibility of which he was proud.

Is Ahab, Ahab Who Provoked the Lord God of Israel?

When we ask the question, Is Ahab (of Nantucket) Ahab (king of Israel), we are actually asking in what way the captain of the *Pequod* resembles the wicked king of the First Book of Kings. In chapter 16, "The Ship," Ishmael told of the peculiarity of Biblical names among Nantucket Quakers. He also speculated that such a name, coupled with the "bold and nervous language" a man learns from solitude with nature, could fashion a being "formed for noble tragedies." Thus, as soon as we learn Captain Ahab's name in the novel, we are instructed to anticipate a tragic appropriateness to it.

The narrator had marshaled typology to give weight to his story in the very first sentence, "Call me Ishmael." He implies that the ad hoc name is more relevant than the one given him at birth. No one in the novel ever addresses him as Ishmael, or by any other name. By stopping the flow of his narrative, as soon as Captains Peleg and Bildad are introduced and Ahab mentioned by name, in order to warn us of the importance of these names, he invites the reader to investigate Scriptural etymology and narrative.

In a useful note Willard Thorp pointed out that Peleg means "division"; Captain Peleg divides the lays of the ship's income. Bildad was one of Job's comforters; like him the co-owner of the *Pequod* spouts warnings against wickedness. Neither of these men is "formed for noble tragedies." The manner in which Ahab will correspond to his Biblical type is not immediately apparent; only a reading of the whole novel will answer that question. "The Ship" whets our interest in Ahab, who will not appear for another twelve chapters.

More is made of his name in this seductive chapter of intimations than of the other Biblical names. Captain Peleg's attempt to minimalize the implications of Ahab's name only makes it more ominous:

> Captain Ahab did not name himself. 'Twas a foolish, ignorant whim of his crazy, widowed mother, who died when he was only a twelvemonth old. And yet the old squaw Tistig, at Gayhead, said that the name would somehow prove prophetic. And, perhaps, other fools like her may tell thee the same. I wish to warn thee. It's a lie.

As an argument for Ahab's humanity, Peleg adds that he has a young wife and a son. These facts will play no role in the novel until "The Symphony."

The sudden appearance in chapter 19 of a prophet, named Elijah, who curses Ahab, almost immediately confirms Peleg's warning. Yet the coincidence of two names from the First Book of Kings erodes the authority of his dismissal of the typological significance. Elijah cryptically refers to blasphemies the captain committed and to a prophecy that had been confirmed by his losing a leg. As soon as Ishmael learns Elijah's name, he repeats it with an exclamation mark.

Encouraged by the correspondence of names from the Scriptural narrative of Ahab's wickedness, the reader will look in vain for a Jezebel. Is Ahab Ahab without Jezebel? Certainly, in this novel virtually devoid of women, a moody leader, with a diabolical cosmology, bringing himself and his crew to destruction would justify the name and fulfill the "somehow" of Tistig's prophecy. Nevertheless, if we read "The Symphony" carefully we may find Jezebel haunting the chapter even though we never hear her name. I do not mean to suggest that the "sweet, resigned girl" Ahab married is a figure for the Sidonian princess. On the contrary, her noncorrespondence to the Biblical narrative seems to guarantee her ineffectiveness in *Moby-Dick*. "The Symphony" dramatizes the impossibility of Ahab's acting on her behalf.

In the chapter's opening paragraph Melville conflates two themes typical of *Moby-Dick,* the reduction of space to an undifferentiated plane and the domination of a single color, and introduces a third, the feminization of a part of the natural world:

> It was a clear steel-blue day. The firmaments of air and sea were hardly separable in that all-pervading azure; only, the pensive air was transparently pure and soft, with a woman's look, and the robust and man-like sea heaved with long, strong, lingering swells as Samson's chest in his sleep.

The reduction of the visible world to an undifferentiated monochromatic plane is the final version of a disorientation of spatiality that began in the dark of New Bedford with Ishmael's stumbling into a Negro church where he caught enough of the sermon to know it was about "the blackness of darkness." The Spouter-Inn's befogged oil painting, which poses the first puzzle for interpretation the narrator faces, and the crucial meditation on blankness in "The Whiteness of the Whale" would be the other moments in this series. The pervading blueness of "The Symphony," then, completes the long-interrupted triad.

This is also the final instance of a more continuous play on color that progressed from the early passages on blackness and whiteness to the chromatic richness of silver ("The Spirit Spout"), yellow ("Brit"), and crimson ("Stubb Kills a Whale") before reaching the lush blindness of blue on blue, a visual equivalent of the riddle of differentiation posed by the question, "Is Ahab, Ahab?"

Against the backdrop of blueness Melville inscribes a parody of Genesis 1. In the opening paragraph the narrator mimes the work of God on the second day: he divides the firmaments. In the subsequent four paragraphs the work of the fifth, fourth, and sixth days, in that order, finds counterparts in the chapter as the creatures of air and sea, the stars, and, lastly, man are represented in the hitherto pervading blueness.

The world is remade in the first paragraphs of "The Symphony" in order to revise the place of woman in the scheme of Genesis. In the alternative cosmology nature itself is sexualized, and copulates. The feminine dimension appears benign and passive in the language of the chapter, but the metaphorical undercurrents suggest an active and destructive femininity. The simile of Samson's chest describes the latent power of the rolling ocean. However, crowding upon this image, comes the unstated allusion to his betrayal by Delilah. The only mention of Samson's sleep in the Old Testament is part of the narrative of her treachery: "And she made him sleep upon her knees; and she called for a man, and she caused him to shave off the seven locks of his head; and she began to afflict him, and his strength went from him" (Judges 16:19).

The subterranean logic of this passage contradicts the literal meaning.

One day in the voyage of the *Pequod* brings to mind the first six days of Creation. The explicitly developed image of masculine sexual conquest of an innocent, gentle woman suggests erotic violence by the "murderous" male; but the simile of Samson brings into play the erotic manipulations of a castrating female. Furthermore, I believe there is a silent symbolical equation of the unnamed Delilah with the unnamed Jezebel.

Melville renders Ahab's ambiguous position in this amorous spectacle with a verbal deviousness that deserves our attention. The fourth and fifth paragraphs postpone their grammatical subjects for seven and twenty-seven words, respectively. In both cases it is possible to anticipate a different subject. First, we might read "Aloft, like a royal czar and king," as if Ahab himself were to be the subject. Instead it is the sun. The previous paragraph, describing the identity of the air and the sea—"it was only the sex, as it were, that distinguished them"—would lead the reader to expect a human agent to be introduced as the figure reading this sexual discrimination into the field of vision. Conversely, the fifth paragraph unreels a long series of past participles, which can be read as a continuation of the description of the elemental lovemaking of the previous paragraph. The words "Tied up and twisted; gnarled and knotted with wrinkles; haggardly firm and unyielding" ambiguously fuse the delayed subject to the previous picture of copulation. The first four words could continue that primal scene unproblematically. Only after a fourteen-word description of his eyes, does the phrase "untottering Ahab" specify the grammatical subject. We do not learn what he is observing, only that he faces "the fair girl's forehead of heaven." The paratactic construction permits us to read Ahab as alternately a participant and an observer in the primal scene of nature, until the grammatical meaning asserts itself, terminating the images of sexual intercourse.

The ambiguity of watching or participating in intercourse frequently characterizes the primal scene in psychoanalytical literature. It is important that Melville not only suggests this oscillation in his text, but he forces the reader into repeating this ambiguous situation in the process of discerning what is happening in the chapter. This strategy volatilizes the undersong of the text. As we focus upon the erotic representation, intimations of more than we can discern through the denotations of the descriptive language direct our attention to the repressed figuration of the narrative. Ahab even comes to represent the reader's problem here.

After a puzzling paragraph, which I shall address shortly, Ahab finally directs his gaze to the sea. Therefore, he has looked at both participants in the sexual scene. But in looking at the sea, "he strove to pierce the profundity." The path to this "profundity" is through his own reflected image.

His narcissistic identification with the male half of the elemental coupling brings him into contact with the contradictory, but unreconciled, images of female as innocent bride and castrating traitor. Although he cannot pierce this profundity, he is shaken by a feeling of the emptiness of his life, which is expressed first by a tear.

Is Ahab Ishmael?

In the preceding discussion I have been reading "The Symphony" as if the narrator, Ishmael, were identical with the author, Melville. The paragraph I mentioned, which comes between the introduction of Ahab and the scene of his gazing at the sea, makes that difficult.

In an apostrophe to the innocence of the air and sky, the narrator asserts his authority within the chapter by inscribing the pronouns "us" and "I." However, the image he uses to personify the "invisible winged creatures" of the air has eluded convincing interpretation:

> But so have I seen little Miriam and Martha, laughing-eyed elves, heedlessly gambol around their old sire; sporting with the circle of singed locks which grew on the marge of that burnt-out crater of his brain.

Charles Feidelson, the most discreet of the commentators, has noted that the reference to Miriam and Martha and their sire is not known. Mansfield and Vincent, at the other end of the editorial spectrum, fantasize that Melville has invented names for Lot's incestuous daughters here. Murray points to the description of Teufelsdröch in Carlyle's *Sartor Resartus*: "as of some silent, high-encircled mountain-pool, perhaps the crater of an extinct volcano, into whose black depths you fear to gaze" (bk. 1, ch. 4) and identifies the innocent figures as Hawthorne's children under pseudonyms. In his fascinating and provocative annotations, Harold Beaver acknowledges some point to the private joke about Hawthorne, adding that Ishmael speaks as if he were Lazarus, recalling a scene of his two sisters. The variety and ingenuity of these glosses underscore the problem.

Not only is the allusion obscure, but the testimony of Ishmael seems unnecessary. None of the editors addresses the *strangeness* of Ishmael's intrusion here. Until "The Symphony," the narrator had not made his presence known by speaking in the first person since "The Candles," thirteen chapters earlier. He will not utter "I" again in the three concluding chapters of the chase of Moby Dick. The first person reemerges, in the "Epilogue," with Ishmael himself, as he accounts for his surprising survival after the whale wrecked the *Pequod*.

Only Beaver notices the presence of the narrator when he annotates this paragraph. If we understand Lot or Hawthorne to be the old sire, then, the declaration, "But so have I seen" only confuses the analogy to Ahab. Referring back to chapter 3, "The Spouter-Inn," Beaver suggests that Ishmael, who already knows the conclusion of the novel as he writes it, identified with Lazarus. But if that is true, who is the old sire? Why does he write "their" not "our" old sire? The New Testament tells us nothing of Lazarus' father. Perhaps the British editors saw the oddity of this passage; they omitted it from *The Whale*.

Although I have no superior reading for the "laughing-eyed elves," I dwell on this passage just because the narrator asserts himself here. What he has seen and what he sees is crucial for a reading of *Moby-Dick*. We should recall that the narrative style shifts decisively after the *Pequod* leaves Nantucket harbor. The intense subjectivity of the first twenty chapters quickly dissolves. Ishmael suddenly begins to ventriloquize conversations and monologues to which the circumscribed narrator of the book's initial chapters would have had no access. The theatrical title of chapter 1, in which this is evident, "Enter Ahab; to Him, Stubb," lends support to Charles Olson's contention that there were two versions of the novel; one centering on the Ishmael-Queequeg relationship; the other, an Ahabiad, written after Melville had immersed himself in Shakespeare. Certainly, the narrator becomes a self-conscious Shakespearean only after boarding the *Pequod*. Even his taxonomy of whales takes the form of Octavos and Folios. Yet, this bookish whalelore emerges with an authority we would not have expected from the landed Ishmael. Moreover, his excursions into fictional omniscience correspond to an abandonment of the timid and often puzzled persona he had so meticulously created in the early pages of the novel. In the middle chapters, vestiges of the initial Ishmael show through those passages where he is in contact with Queequeg.

As the narrative progresses there is a further loss of Ishmael's voice. The final thirty chapters have little or nothing of the scholarly whalelore that dominated the sixty before them. The most obvious consequence of this negligence of self-portraiture is the collapse of the vivid distinction between Ishmael's mind and Ahab's. Of course, that had been the point of the brilliant essay in intellectual temperament, "The Whiteness of the Whale," where, shortly after seeing Ahab for the first time and hearing of the quest for the white whale, Ishmael talked himself into a terror over the Emersonian theme of "the blank we see when we look on nature."

The last, pale glimpse we get of Ishmael's mind in action occurs in "The Pacific." The long-awaited balm of the Pacific Ocean almost restores his spirits as he tries to shake off the implications of the previous chapter, "Queequeg in His Coffin." The sea itself, "my dear Pacific," becomes for him a tomb and bed of the dreaming dead. Its rhythms quickly seduce him into worship of Pan, at one and the same time a deity of eros and the cause of unexplained panic to the travellers who encounter him. In that final measuring of the intellectual distance between Ahab and himself, Ishmael records how the captain was untouched by the enthusiasm he felt. In fact, "The Pacific" is the precursor of "The Symphony." But in the latter the narrator's consciousness fuses with that of Ahab's.

The intrusion of the first person singular into "The Symphony" reminds us that the description of the azure world in the opening paragraphs had been through his eyes. Whenever the narrator writes "I" or "Ahab" in *Moby-Dick* he performs a straightforward act of representation; a sailor or the captain comes into the reader's "view." Those same two words, in Ahab's mouth, are extremely problematic. Ahab's grandiose sense of his own name forecloses the possibility of his telling his own story. When Ishmael describes the world as he encounters it in his fictional persona, there is always a possibility that his neurotic obsessions, which he himself called his "hypos" (slang for hypochondriac delusions) in the opening chapter, inflect or even distort his perceptions. The most massive of his hypos is his reaction to whiteness. Perhaps we can read the chapters in theatrical form as marked off from the blinders of his hypos. They begin to appear shortly before the meditation on whiteness.

Ishmael is almost as obsessed with blueness as he is with whiteness. In chapter 35, "The Mast-Head," he attributes that color to the soul. He describes how the meditative sailor on watch in the mast-head endangers his life by losing himself in thought: he "takes the mystic ocean at his feet for the visible image of the deep, blue, bottomless soul, pervading mankind and nature; and every strange halfseen, gliding, beautiful thing that eludes him; every dimly-discovered, uprising fin of some undiscernible form, seems to him the embodiment of those elusive thoughts that only people the soul by continually flitting through it." Furthermore, in "Queequeg in His Coffin," he portrays the pagan's idea of heaven in terms of blue and white: "for not only do they believe that the stars are isles, but that far beyond all visible horizons, their own mild, uncontinented seas, interflow with blue heavens; and so form the white breakers of the milky way."

The opening of "The Symphony" is not only a description of a day in the Pacific. It is implicitly a representation of how Ishmael reacted to the "hardly separable" layers of blue and how he read Creation into it, along with the troubled undersong of female violence. As early as "Loomings" he had confessed an identification with Narcissus. In "The Mast-Head" he comically acknowledged the threatening power of that identification. Ruminating "Pantheists" aloft in the mast feel how the "identity comes back in horror" when they let a foot slip and plunge to death. In fact, much later, in "The Life-Buoy," an anonymous crew member falls from his watch post, his body unrecovered. The description of this "falling phantom" echos "the ungraspable phantom of life" that all Narcissuses seek according to the philosopher of "Loomings." Finally, the only vestiges of the fallen watchman were "white bubbles in the blue of the sea."

Restoring Ishmael to his role as Narcissistic gazer at the beginning of "The Symphony" does not necessitate displacing Ahab. Ishmael reminds us he is there only *after* the scene has been painted. This is a ploy in paragraph arrangement that repeats the strategy of withholding the grammatical subject in two successive, paragraph-long sentences. Ishmael had been forgotten at the beginning of the chapter. Contextual clues point us to read the opening description as if it mimed Ahab's perceptions. Only retrospectively do we learn they were Ishmael's. The effect is a fusion of the two figures. Here the narrator disposes of the accustomed antithesis of "I" and "Ahab."

Not only does he transfer the Narcissus type from himself to the captain by portraying him as he "watched how his shadow in the water sank and sank to his gaze," he adds two other images as well, which had been used to define Ishmael's mentality. They are orphanhood and live burial. The very first mention of sleep in the novel and the earliest menacing woman were evoked when the narrator found himself in Queequeg's embrace. He recalled a punishment inflicted by his stepmother on the summer solstice. In an intermediate state between dreaming and waking, cruelly confined to his bed, he had the uncanny sense of a "supernatural hand" in his. When Ahab drops a tear into the ocean, experiencing the Panic epiphany that Ishmael knew twenty-one chapters before, he is embraced by "the step-mother world," another female image for the mild air. The word "step-mother" reminds us that the mad mother who named Ahab died in his infancy. Yet, the only stepmother in the book is Ishmael's. This term smuggles a sinister note into the superficially benign moment and brings Ahab another step closer to Ishmael.

The third image transferred from Ishmael's psychic history to Ahab is that of Adam buried under time. In the Whaleman's Chapel, the markers for men lost at sea re-inspired the narrator's reverie of paralysis: "in what eternal, unstirring paralysis, and deadly, hopeless trance, yet lies antique

Adam who died sixty round centuries ago." Ahab, in turn, confesses to Starbuck, who saw him drop his tear into the sea, that he feels "as though I were Adam, staggering beneath the piled centuries since Paradise." Then he breaks into a Lear-like cry to be annihilated.

The transference of Ishmael's hypos to Ahab prepares the way for the complete divestment of the narrating persona in the book. The final three chapters, the only ones in which Moby-Dick appears, have no traces of Ishmael. In fact, when he resurfaces on Queequeg's coffin in the "Epilogue," Ishmael provides the astonishing news that "I was he . . . who, when on the last day three men were tossed from out of the rocking boat, was dropped astern." This is astonishing simply because he had written, in the neutral third person, of an unnamed "third man" falling overboard. This is the most blatant of the retrospective admissions of the narrator. When he does, at last, plunge to his predicted fate as a modern Narcissus, we do not see him, nor does he really drown.

We know that Melville wrote the end of the novel in a feverish rush; the epilogue and two paragraphs of "The Symphony" were among the passages that do not appear in the British edition, which preceded the American. However, haste and sloppiness do not account for the disguise of Ishmael in the finale. Something more is at stake. There is a deliberate gesture of calling our attention to the loss of the first-person voice by the end of the book. Even the phrase "I was he" reflects, on the level of grammar, the fated substitution of Ishmael from the otherwise unknown bowsman, who, replacing the dead Fedallah, left a position to be filled. In a sense Ishmael does die: "I" becomes "he." He does not, like Pip, lose the capability of saying both I and his own name, after falling into the sea. He has already lost his name and his autonarrating authority in the final chapters. The epilogue restores both to him. But before that he was buried as the "third" person—Melville wrote "third man"—when he was lost.

Is Ahab Fedallah?

The two blue fields, air and water, are projections of sexual difference on what Ahab called "the pasteboard mask" of the visible world. Its imminent blankness generated Ishmael's horror and Ahab's violent, Oedipal quest. Starbuck, who lacks the Emersonian absolutism of either Ishmael or Ahab, attempts to divert the tragic conclusion by promoting the differences emerging in the seascape. He humanizes and idealizes the female figures, otherwise virtually expelled from the novel.

Earlier he had failed as an imitator of Ahab. His monologue in the chapter called "The Musket" brings his own wife's name—Mary—into the text for the first time. But even the thought of her and of his son cannot bring him to murder the captain. Thinking back to the oath on the Quarter Deck, he realizes that his mutiny would earn him the name of Ahab. He rejects that option: "Aye, and say'st the men have vowed thy vow; say'st all of us are Ahabs. Great God forbid!"

When "the stepmother world" coaxed a tear from Ahab, breaking his Narcissus-like trance, Starbuck approached him. In the ensuing dialogue, he vainly attempted to convince the captain to abort his quest and sail for Nantucket. For a moment, the mate seemed to penetrate Ahab's solipsism. The captain was attracted by the mirroring of his first mate's eyes: "Let me look into a human eye; it is better than to gaze into sea or sky; better than to gaze upon God." Sea and sky stand for sexualized nature here; coming face to face with God has the Mosaic consequence of death, as a careful reader of chapter 86 would know. In facing Starbuck, Ahab turns from the primal scene of nature and from his Oedipal rage at the apotheosized whale toward a domestic humanism that cannot satisfy him.

In Starbuck's eyes Ahab sees his own shunned family. Rather than divert his course, he urges the mate to remain on board when the boats are lowered to chase Moby-Dick. The dialogue they share does not affect the drama. The narrator compares it to an apple of Sodom, drawing his allusion from *Paradise Lost*, according to all the annotators. This vegetative image of delusive nourishment actually completes the very first portrait of Ahab the narrator drew at the end of chapter 28. There an allegorical figure pictures April and May as tripping "dancing girls" (like elfin Martha and Miriam later) returning to "the wintry, misanthropic woods," where even the strongest "thunder-cloven oak" would respond to them by sending "forth some few green sprouts, to welcome such glad-hearted visitants; so Ahab did, in the end, a little respond to the playful alluring of the girlish air."

In *Moby-Dick* dialogue itself leaves cinders in the mouth of advocates of reason. No characters are more fit for verbal exchange than Starbuck and Ahab, yet this is the only moment in which meaningful discussion even seems possible. Nor can Ahab speak fruitfully to the captain of the Samuel Enderby, who lost his arm to the white whale. The intimate companions Ishmael and Queequeg are constrained by the latter's "broken phraseology" and many incomprehensible words. Fedallah speaks oracularly to Ahab; he, in turn, misconstrues the sense of Fedallah's words as fatally as Macbeth the rhymes of the witches. Stubb sadistically forces the old black cook, Fleece, to preach to sharks or "diddles" the French-speaking captain of the

Rose Bud (itself a ribald joke about female sexual anatomy) out of ambergris through an interpreter. Neither the carpenter nor the blacksmith truly converses with Ahab; they respond to his monologues. Of course, Ahab prefers monologue. He keeps Pip by his side after the cabinboy had seen "God's foot upon the treadle of the loom, and spoke it" in a schizophrenic idiolect without control over his name or the first person pronoun. Pip's eyes, as well, suit Ahab because he does not see his "reflection in the vacant pupils."

The voices of *Moby-Dick* are heard in sermons, formal tales of the adventures of ships encountered at sea, pandemonian rallies in the cult of white-whale hatred, and, above all, in monologues, which increase in frequency in the final section of the book, once Ishmael has completed his inventory of the ship and his whalelore.

At the end of "The Symphony" the reader feels the predominance of monologue over dialogue when he learns, again after the fact, that Starbuck had "stolen away" during Ahab's climactic rumination on fate. This delayed revelation necessarily identifies us with the monomaniacal Ahab; we are bound by his speech even when no one else is listening; like Ahab, we do not realize we are alone. In this manner, the shift of emphasis from a language controlled by Ishmael to one articulated by Ahab finds a dramatic form.

The speech itself contains a drift of tone. From the high rhetoric of the opening questions that try to displace responsibility for the deadly quest from Ahab to a god of fate, the monologue comes to speak of the naturalization of predatory instincts. God and man become consubstantial through murder. Finally, it beautifully trails off with a pastoral image that reinterprets the softening force of the weather. Eliminating the sexuality of the opening paragraphs, unless a faint trace of Samson can be detected in the picture of the mowers sleeping in hay, Ahab tortures himself with a parable about the destructive power of time. The sleeping mowers have not been given enough time to complete their appointed task. In their deathly sleep there is also an echo of his own castrative scar: "Sleep, Aye, and rust amid greenness; as last year's scythes flung down, and left in half-cut swaths."

Ultimately the erotic softening engendered by the imagined intercourse of sea and air brings home to Ahab his fateful crippling. He fancies the reapers are asleep "somewhere under the slopes of the Andes." The mild wind, then, blows from the symbolic world of the doubloon, nailed to the mast for the man who first sights Moby-Dick. Of course, that will be Ahab himself. The coin, as he interpreted it, showed "Ahab . . . Ahab . . . Ahab . . . Ahab." His interrupted attempt to penetrate the profundity brings him to a depth somewhere under Ahab.

Throughout the novel, the depths of Ahab's mind are associated with the ghostly Fedallah. Before Fedallah made his first appearance, Ishmael had compared "the larger, darker, deeper part" of Ahab's mind to the Roman baths under the Hotel de Cluny where a "captive king" upholds "on his frozen brow the piled entablatures of ages." Fedallah gives Ahab what he most needs, the assurance that he will not be undone by time. Rather, Ahab takes that assurance by reading Fedallah's prophecy to his own advantage. When he completes his speech and notices that Starbuck has departed, he goes back to studying his image in the sea-mirror:

> Ahab crossed the deck to gaze over on the other side; but he
> started at two reflected, fixed eyes in the water there. Fedallah
> was motionlessly leaning over the same rail.

In the end of "The Symphony," as again and again within it, we have to read backwards. The eyes Ahab sees reflected are his shadowy harpooner's. But here the final sentence is poised ambiguously. We can read the conclusion as Ahab startled by his own fixed eyes with Fedallah monitoring him. Then again, if both sets of eyes are superimposed on the same reflecting surface, we find ourselves in the now familiar but still disturbing realm of what is "hardly separable." They are eyes without a name.

Chronology

1819	Herman Melville (or Melvill) born August 1 in New York City. He is the third child of Allan Melville, an importer, and Maria Gansevoort Melville.
1826	Melville attends the New-York Male High School.
–32	Allan Melville's importing business fails, and he moves the family to Albany. Herman becomes a student at the Albany Academy until his father's death in 1832. Then he works at various jobs: bank clerk, helper on his brother Gansevoort's farm, assistant in Gansevoort's fur factory and store.
38	Continues his education at various high schools, supplementing the family income by teaching at a district school.
39	"Fragments from a Writing Desk" published May 4 and May 18 in the *Democratic Press and Lansingburgh Advertiser*. Melville then works his way to Liverpool and back on the *Saint Lawrence*, a merchant ship.
841–44	Melville leaves New Bedford, Massachusetts, as a sailor on the whaler *Acushnet*, bound for the South Seas. Jumps ship in the Marquesas Islands, where he lives among the natives for about a month. After a series of adventures, travels home as a passenger on the frigate *United States*.
1846	Publishes *Typee*. Brother Gansevoort dies.
1847	Publishes *Omoo*. Marries Elizabeth Shaw, daughter of Chief Justice Lemuel Shaw of Boston.
1847–50	Melville tries to earn a living as a writer, producing occasional articles and reviews. Makes acquaintance of George and Evert Duyckinck, and other New York literary figures.
1849	Publishes *Mardi* and *Redburn*. Travels to Europe. Son Malcolm born.

1850	Publishes *White-Jacket*. Purchases Arrowhead, a farm near Pittsfield, Massachusetts. Begins his friendship with Nathaniel Hawthorne, who lives in nearby Lenox.
1851	Publishes *Moby-Dick*. Son Stanwix born.
1852	Publishes *Pierre*.
1853	Daughter Elizabeth born.
1853–56	Writes stories and sketches for *Putnam's Monthly Magazine* and *Harper's New Monthly Magazine*.
1855	Publishes *Israel Potter* as a book, after serialization in *Putnam's*. Daughter Frances born.
1856	*The Piazza Tales* published. Melville travels to Europe and the Near East for his health.
1857	*The Confidence-Man*, which Melville had left with his publisher before he began travelling, is finally published. Melville returns to the United States.
1857–60	Melville supports family by lectures on such topics as "Statues in Rome," "The South Seas," and "Traveling."
1863	Melville sells Arrowhead, and moves his family to New York City.
1866	Publishes a collection of poems, *Battle-Pieces and Aspects of the War*.
1867	Son Malcolm shoots himself, after which son Stanwix runs away to sea.
1876	Publishes *Clarel*.
1886	Son Stanwix dies.
1888	*John Marr and Other Sailors* privately printed.
1891	*Timoleon* privately printed. Melville dies on September 28.
1924	First publication of *Billy Budd, Sailor*.

Contributors

HAROLD BLOOM, Sterling Professor of the Humanities at Yale University, is the author of *The Anxiety of Influence*, *Poetry and Repression*, and many other volumes of literary criticism. His forthcoming study, *Freud: Transference and Authority*, attempts a full-scale reading of all of Freud's major writings. A MacArthur Prize Fellow, he is general editor of five series of literary criticism published by Chelsea House.

CHARLES OLSON, considered by many to have been the major poet of his American generation, is remembered most for his *Maximus Poems*.

DAVID SIMPSON is Professor of English at Northwestern University. His books include *Irony and Authority in Romantic Poetry* and *Wordsworth and the Figurings of the Real*.

ROWLAND A. SHERRILL is Assistant Professor of religious studies and English at Indiana University/Purdue University in Indianapolis.

BERT BENDER teaches in the English Department at Arizona State University.

LOUISE K. BARNETT teaches in the English Department at Rutgers University. She is the author of *Ignoble Savage: American Literary Racism, 1790–1890* and *Swift's Poetic Worlds*.

FRANK G. NOVAK, JR., is a member of the Department of Communications at Pepperdine University.

P. ADAMS SITNEY teaches film and literature at Princeton University and is the author of *Visionary Film*. He has also edited several volumes of film criticism and the literary essays of Maurice Blanchot.

Bibliography

Arvin, Newton. *Herman Melville*. New York: William Sloane Associates, 1950.

Beaver, Harold. "Melville and Modernism." *Dutch Quarterly Review of Anglo-American Letters* 13, no. 1 (1983): 1–15.

Berthoff, Warner. *The Example of Melville*. Princeton: Princeton University Press, 1962.

Bowen, Merlin. *The Long Encounter*. Chicago: The University of Chicago Press, 1963.

Brodhead, R. H. *Hawthorne, Melville and the Novel*. Chicago: The University of Chicago Press, 1976.

Brodtkorb, Paul. *Ishmael's White World*. New Haven: Yale University Press, 1967.

Cook, Charles H., Jr. "Ahab's 'Intolerable Allegory.' " *Boston University Studies in English* 1 (1955–56): 45–52.

Dryden, Edgar A. *Melville's Thematics of Form*. Baltimore: The Johns Hopkins University Press, 1968.

Edinger, Edward A. *Melville's Moby Dick: A Jungian Commentary*. New York: New Directions, 1978.

Egan, P. J. "Time and Ishmael's Character in the Town-Ho's Story of *Moby-Dick*." *Studies in the Novel* 14 (1983): 337–47.

Feidelson, Charles, Jr. *Symbolism and American Literature*. Chicago: The University of Chicago Press, 1953.

Fiedler, Leslie. *Love and Death in the American Novel*. New York: Stein and Day, 1966.

Greenberg, R. M. "The 3-Day Chase—Multiplicity and Coherence in *Moby-Dick*." *ESQ—Journal of the American Renaissance* 29 (1983): 91–98.

Kazin, Alfred. "An Introduction to *Moby-Dick*." Introduction to *Moby-Dick*. Boston: Houghton Mifflin Company, 1956.

Lawrence, D. H. "Moby Dick, or the White Whale." In *Studies in Classic American Literature*. New York: Thomas Seltzer, Inc., 1923.

Lee, A. Robert. "*Moby-Dick:* The Tale and the Telling." *New Perspectives on Melville*, edited by Faith Pullin. Kent, Ohio: Kent State University Press, 1978.

Lewis, R. W. B. *The American Adam*. Chicago: The University of Chicago Press, 1955.

Leyda, Jay. *The Melville Log*. 2 vols. New York: Harcourt, Brace, 1951.

Matthiessen, F. O. *American Renaissance*. New York: Oxford University Press, 1941.

Mumford, Lewis. *Herman Melville.* New York: Harcourt Brace and Company, 1929.

Parker, Hershel and Harrison Hayford, eds. *Moby-Dick as Doubloon.* New York: W. W. Norton, 1970.

Patterson, M. R. "Democratic Leadership and Narrative Authority in *Moby-Dick.*" *Studies in the American Novel* 16 (1984): 288–303.

Rogin, Michael Paul. *Subversive Genealogy.* Berkeley: University of California Press, 1979.

Rosenberry, Edward H. *Melville.* Boston: Routledge and Kegan Paul, 1979.

———. *Melville and the Comic Spirit.* Cambridge: Harvard University Press, 1955.

Sedgwick, William Ellery. *The Tragedy of Mind.* Cambridge: Harvard University Press, 1944.

Sewall, Richard B. *The Vision of Tragedy.* New Haven: Yale University Press, 1959.

Stern, Milton R. *The Fine Hammered Steel of Herman Melville.* Urbana: University of Illinois Press, 1968.

Vincent, Howard P. *The Trying-Out of Moby-Dick.* Boston: Houghton Mifflin Company, 1949.

Watters, R. E. "The Meanings of the White Whale." *University of Toronto Quarterly* 20 (1951): 155–68.

Zoellner, Robert. *The Salt Sea Mastodon.* Berkeley: University of California Press, 1973.

Acknowledgments

"Call Me Ishmael" by Charles Olson from *Call Me Ishmael* by Charles Olson, ©
1947 by Charles Olson, renewed 1973 by the Estate of Charles Olson. Reprinted
by permission of the Estate of Charles Olson.

" 'In Nomine Diaboli': *Moby-Dick*" (originally entitled "In Nomine Diaboli") by
Henry A. Murray from *New England Quarterly* 24 (December 1951), © 1951
by *New England Quarterly*. Reprinted by permission of *New England Quarterly*.

"Herman Melville: Chasing the Whale" by David Simpson from *Fetishism and
Imagination: Dickens, Melville, Conrad* by David Simpson, © 1982 by David
Simpson. Reprinted by permission of the Johns Hopkins University Press.

"The Career of Ishmael's Self-Transcendence" (originally entitled "The Span of
Portents: The Career of Ishmael's Self-Transcendence") by Rowland A. Sherrill
from *The Prophetic Melville: Experience, Transcendence and Tragedy* by Rowland
A. Sherrill, © 1979 by the University of Georgia Press. Reprinted by permission
of the University of Georgia Press.

"*Moby-Dick*, An American Lyrical Novel" by Bert Bender from *Studies in the Novel*
10, no. 3 (Fall 1978), © 1978 by North Texas State University. Reprinted by
permission.

"Speech in *Moby-Dick*" by Louise K. Barnett from *Studies in American Fiction* 2, no.
2 (Autumn 1983), © 1983 by Northeastern University. Reprinted by
permission.

"The Metaphysics of Beauty and Terror in *Moby-Dick*" (originally entitled
" 'Warmest Climes but Nurse the Cruellest Fangs': The Metaphysics of Beauty
and Terror in *Moby-Dick*") by Frank G. Novak, Jr., from *Studies in the Novel*
15, no. 4 (Winter 1983), © 1983 by North Texas State University. Reprinted by
permission.

"Ahab's Name: A Reading of 'The Symphony' " by P. Adams Sitney, © 1985 by
P. Adams Sitney. Printed by permission of Georges Borchardt, Inc.

Index